# A MICHIGAN Guide

# Step Up to the TOEFL® iBT for Intermediate Students

### NIGEL A. CAPLAN

Series Editor
LAWRENCE J. ZWIER

Ann Arbor
University of Michigan

Copyright © by the University of Michigan 2009
All rights reserved
Published in the United States of America
The University of Michigan Press
Manufactured in the United States of America

⊗ Printed on acid-free paper

ISBN-13: 978-0-472-03285-3

2012    2011    2010    2009              4        3        2        1

The test directions and sample questions printed in this book are not actual TOEFL® iBT test materials. Training materials and other testing information are provided in their entirety by the University of Michigan  Press. No endorsement of this publication by Educational Testing Service should be inferred.

# Series Preface

Success on the TOEFL® Internet-based Test (iBT) depends on skills that the iBT does not directly test. In particular, aspiring iBT candidates need practice with English grammar, vocabulary, and pronunciation. It is possible to practice these basics incidentally by working with typical iBT-preparation books, but only if you are already close to TOEFL® competence. Otherwise, the preparation books will simply be too hard. It's a circular problem: You can't practice the basics because you haven't got enough competence in the basics. The books in the University of Michigan Press's *Step Up* series are meant for students whose grammar, vocabulary, and pronunciation skills are not yet sufficient for full-scale TOEFL® preparation. As the title indicates, we are hoping to provide platforms from which a pre-TOEFL® student can work toward earnest preparation for the test.

Grammar instruction is at the foundation of *Step Up*, the platform on which vocabulary and pronunciation lessons are set. The selection of grammar points for each unit has been determined by functions commonly elicited on the iBT. For example, the writing and speaking sections of the iBT are likely to ask a test-taker to express preferences and opinions. Unit 6 addresses modals of suggestion/necessity and real conditionals because these features are very handy in such expressions. The vocabulary and pronunciation topics in Unit 6 proceed from the same iBT-related function and relate closely to the grammar points. Of course, the expression of preferences and opinions is likely to figure into passages for the reading and listening sections of the iBT as well.

As currently planned, the *Step Up* series will include at least two volumes: basic and intermediate. Nigel A. Caplan's intermediate volume appears first in the series. This is meant for students who are not too far from handling the English on the iBT—but who are not quite there. This volume pauses to explain lexico-syntactic features of English that are taken as understood in most iBT-prep books. It offers practice in language points that, though basic, may not be firmly under control by students planning to take the test.

The vocabulary used in this intermediate volume may seem at times a bit advanced, even iBT-like. This is necessary and fitting for many reasons. As experienced teachers of English for Academic Purposes know very well, even grammatically shaky students can post significant gains in receptive vocabulary. Progress in this area helps ratchet forward the student's exposure to grammatically diverse discourse and serious, substantive texts, like those on the iBT.

Seriousness and substance are constant attributes of the texts in the *Step Up* series.

Just as philosophers since Cicero have noted that personal virtue entails gravitas—the ability to be taken seriously—so students look for a certain no-nonsense quality in TOEFL®-prep materials. This does not mean the practice passages are dour and inaccessible, but it does mean they can claim topical significance. The iBT entertains only academic content, so there's no point in setting a TOEFL®-prep course by any other lights.

This goes deeper than so-called face validity. Yes, tone is part of it. It is important for students to believe that even a basic-skills textbook treats them with respect; their motivation is likely to rest on that belief. The real test, however, is in whether students are more viable candidates for the iBT after using *Step Up*. We are confident they will be, and we hope you enjoy traveling with them in that direction.

—Lawrence J. Zwier, Series Editor

Grateful acknowledgment is given to the following individuals for lending their voices to the audio: Jay Banerjee, Lindsay Devine, Pat Grimes, Badria Jazairi, and Jeremy Sobczak.

# Contents

*Scope and Sequence*                                                    viii

*To the Teacher*                                                         ix

*To the Student*                                                         xii

## Unit 1:  Chronology and Sequences                                    1

Getting Started                                                          1

Grammar You Can Use                                                      2

   *Simple Present and Present Progressive Tenses*       2

   *Simple Past and Past Progressive Tenses*             5

Vocabulary You Need                                                      8

   *Time Signposts*                                      8

   *Process Signposts*                                   10

   *Words to Learn*                                      12

Speaking Clearly                                                        12

   *Contractions*                                        12

   *–ed Endings*                                         13

## Unit 2:  Similarities and Differences                                15

Getting Started                                                         15

Grammar You Can Use                                                     16

   *Comparatives*                                        16

   *Conjunctions*                                        19

Vocabulary You Need                                                     22

   *Similarity Signposts*                                22

   *Difference Signposts*                                23

   *Words to Learn*                                      25

Speaking Clearly                                                        26

   *Using Stress to Show Contrast*                       26

   *Reduced Vowels*                                      27

## Unit 3:  Developing Ideas                                            29

Getting Started                                                         29

Grammar You Can Use                                                     30

   *Pronouns*                                            30

   *Sentence Connectors*                                 33

Vocabulary You Need                                           37
   *Development Signposts*                     37
   *Synonyms*                                  39
   *Words to Learn*                            41
Speaking Clearly                                              41
   *Thought Groups*                            41
   *Major Stress*                              43

**Unit 4:  Cause, Effect, and Correlation**                  45

Getting Started                                               45
Grammar You Can Use                                           46
   *Present Perfect Tense*                     46
   *Future Verb Forms*                         49
Vocabulary You Need                                           53
   *Cause-and-Effect Signposts*               53
   *Cause or Correlation?*                     56
   *Words to Learn*                            58
Speaking Clearly                                              58
   *Reductions*                                58
   *Linking*                                   59

**Unit 5:  Problems and Solutions**                          61

Getting Started                                               61
Grammar You Can Use                                           62
   *Modals of Certainty*                       62
   *Adverbs*                                   65
Vocabulary You Need                                           69
   *Problem Signposts*                         69
   *Solution Signposts*                        71
   *Words to Learn*                            74
Speaking Clearly                                              75
   Can *and* Can't                             75
   *Intonation in Lists*                       76

**Unit 6:  Preferences and Opinions**                        78

Getting Started                                               78
Grammar You Can Use                                           79
   *Modals of Suggestion and Necessity*        79
   *Real Conditionals*                         83

Vocabulary You Need                                                    86
    *Opinion Signposts (Giving Your Opinion)*                          86
    *Hedging and Softening Signposts*                                  89
    *Words to Learn*                                                   92
Speaking Clearly                                                       93
    *Using Intonation to Show Attitude*                                93
    *Discourse Signposts* (um, ah, *and* wow)                          94

**Unit 7:  Paraphrasing**                                             96

Getting Started                                                        96
Grammar You Can Use                                                    97
    *Adjective Clauses*                                                97
    *Subject-Verb Agreement*                                          102
Vocabulary You Need                                                   104
    *Definition Signposts*                                            104
    *Paraphrasing Techniques*                                         107
    *Words to Learn*                                                  110
Speaking Clearly                                                      111
    *Pauses in Adjective Clauses*                                     111
    *–s Endings*                                                      113

**Unit 8:  Sources of Information**                                  115

Getting Started                                                       115
Grammar You Can Use                                                   116
    *Reported Speech*                                                 116
    *Possessives*                                                     119
Vocabulary You Need                                                   121
    *Source Signposts*                                                121
    *Opinion Signposts (Describing Other People's Opinions)*          123
    *Words to Learn*                                                  126
Speaking Clearly                                                      126
    *Pronouncing the* th *sound*                                      126
    *Asking Questions*                                                128

*Appendix A:* Common Irregular Verbs                                  132
*Appendix B:* Contractions                                           134
*Appendix C:* Pronouns                                               135
*Vocabulary Index*                                                    136
*Answer Key*                                                          140
*Audio Transcripts*                                                  168

# Scope and Sequence

| Unit | Function | Grammar | Vocabulary | Pronunciation |
|------|----------|---------|------------|---------------|
| 1 | Chronology and sequences | Simple present and progressive tenses Simple past and progressive tenses | Time signposts Process signposts | Contractions Endings with –ed |
| 2 | Similarities and differences | Comparatives Conjunctions | Similarity signposts Difference signposts | Using stress to show contrast Reduced vowels |
| 3 | Developing ideas | Pronouns Sentence connectors | Development signposts Synonyms | Thought groups Major stress |
| 4 | Cause, effect, and correlation | Present perfect tense Talking about the future | Cause-and-effect signposts Cause or correlation? | Reductions Linking |
| 5 | Problems and solutions | Modals of certainty Adverbs | Problem signposts Solution signposts | Pronunciation of can / can't Intonation in lists |
| 6 | Preferences and opinions | Modals of suggestion and necessity Real conditionals | Opinion signposts (giving your opinion) Hedging and softening signposts | Using intonation to show attitude Discourse signposts (um, ah, and wow) |
| 7 | Paraphrasing | Adjective clauses Subject-verb agreement | Definition signposts Paraphrasing techniques | Pauses in non-restrictive adjective clauses Endings with –s |
| 8 | Sources of information | Reported speech Possessives | Source signposts Opinion signposts (other people's opinions) | Pronouncing the /th/ sound Asking questions |

# To the Teacher

## Introduction

*Step Up to the TOEFL® iBT for Intermediate Students* is a skills-based textbook that helps low to mid-intermediate students prepare to take a **step up** toward the Test of English as a Foreign Language (TOEFL). This is not a test-preparation book: instead, it teaches some of the **grammar, vocabulary, and pronunciation** skills necessary to successfully use a TOEFL®-level preparation book, such as *The Michigan Guide to English for Academic Success and Better TOEFL® Test Scores.*

The Internet-based Test (iBT) assumes a high level of linguistic competency, and many students may not have the language skills necessary to follow a test-preparation book or to attempt the reading, writing, listening, and speaking tasks on the test. Therefore, *Step Up to the TOEFL® iBT* focuses on the underlying abilities that students will need before they prepare to take the test. Specifically, students learn key grammar points of academic English, high-frequency vocabulary (both content and function words) that may occur on the test or be useful in the productive sections of the test, and pronunciation skills that will improve listening and speaking ability. Although the iBT does not directly score grammar, vocabulary, and pronunciation, weaknesses in these areas will severely impair students' performance on all areas of the test. Therefore, every point covered in this textbook will benefit test-takers on one or more sections of the iBT.

## Unit Tour

Each of the eight units addresses one rhetorical function and includes:

- learning targets and their relevance to the four sections of the test
- two **Grammar You Can Use** topics that strengthen students' receptive and productive language
- samples of test-level use of the grammar from *The Michigan Guide to English for Academic Success and Better TOEFL® Test Scores*
- two **Vocabulary You Need** sections highlighting common language functions seen on the iBT
- a list of high-frequency and useful **Words to Learn** from the unit
- two **Speaking Clearly** points focusing on comprehension and fluent delivery
- **Skill-Building Exercises** that practice the language point through high-interest reading, writing, listening, and speaking activities

- **iBT Practice Exercises** that give students practice using the language point in tasks similar to those on the test (including the integrated speaking and writing tasks) but at their level of competency
- **Step Up Notes** with useful hints and tips about stepping up to the TOEFL®.

## Grammar You Can Use

Since the Educational Testing Service has removed the discrete grammar test from the TOEFL®, it is no longer useful to study grammar rules and exceptions as a form of preparation for the test. However, it is also unrealistic for low-intermediate learners to study every possible grammar structure in English. As a result, *Step Up to the TOEFL®* focuses on grammar points that express the language **function** of the unit, are often difficult for learners, and/or increase the complexity of students' production.

The **Grammar You Can Use** sections do not provide the final word on these grammar points. Most areas of English grammar can be studied in increasing depth at higher levels (for example, Unit 7 only discusses subject adjective clauses; object clauses and objects of prepositions are reserved for future study). The goal of this book is to give students the confidence to understand these structures and use them accurately in order to step up to the next level of proficiency.

## Vocabulary You Need

The distinction between grammar and vocabulary is an artificial one, and this text shows learners the connections between grammar structures and the words that fit them. The vocabulary topics are therefore connected to the grammar structures in that they all serve the function of the unit. For example, verbs describing effects are often used in the present perfect tense (Unit 4). By studying the vocabulary in these sections, students will solidify their general vocabulary and begin to develop their academic vocabulary.

Some words from the grammar and vocabulary sections of each unit appear in the **Words to Learn** list. These words have been selected because they are either: (1) high-frequency content words from the General Service List (West 1953); (2) commonly occurring words in university English from the Academic Word List (Coxhead 2000); or (3) useful words for talking about higher education. According to vocabulary experts, students need to learn a basic vocabulary of the General Service List and the Academic Word List plus area-specific content words (Nation 2001). The TOEFL® no longer specifically tests vocabulary knowledge, but it assumes competence in this basic vocabulary.

To use the **Words to Learn** list, students can be asked to search for the use of the item in the unit and study it in more detail. For instance, they could work out the word class (noun, verb, adjective, adverb, etc.), look up a definition, write the sentence from the textbook, or create an original sentence.

## Speaking Clearly

The main focus of this section is improving students' delivery score on the speaking section of the iBT by highlighting learnable features of English prosody and pronunciation. Students use the accompanying audio CD as a model to improve their fluency. If possible, it is beneficial for learners to record their voices using a computer, voice recorder, or cassette player. Teachers and students can then compare the recording to the models and easily see areas of strength and weakness.

### *A Word about the Listening Exercises*

Test-takers can only listen to each lecture and conversation once on the TOEFL®. In class or for self-study, learners studying this book are encouraged to listen more than once to most exercises for practice. However, to simulate the test conditions more closely, they can be restricted to one playback of the recording.

I hope you enjoy teaching *Step Up to the TOEFL® iBT,* and I wish your students good luck as they prepare for the test and their future studies!

—Nigel A. Caplan

## References

Coxhead, A. "The New Academic Word List." *TESOL Quarterly, 34,* no. 2 (2000): 213–38.

Nation, I.S.P. *Learning Vocabulary in Another Language.* New York: Cambridge University Press, 2001.

West, M. *A General Service List of English Words.* London: Longman, 1953.

# To the Student

If you've already taken the Internet-based Test (iBT) or if you've tried to use a TOEFL® preparation textbook, then you already know the language on the test is very difficult. The readings and listenings are in an academic style and discuss complex academic subjects. The grading of the writing and speaking sections is also tough: you need a lot of vocabulary, good grammar, and clear delivery to score well.

*Step Up to the TOEFL® iBT for Intermediate Students* is a skills-based textbook that will help you prepare to take a **step up** toward the Test of English as a Foreign Language. This is not a test-preparation book: instead, it teaches some of the **grammar, vocabulary, and pronunciation** skills you will need for the TOEFL®. After finishing this book, you might be ready to use a TOEFL®-preparation book, such as *The Michigan Guide to English for Academic Success and Better TOEFL® Test Scores*.

In this book, you are going to learn key grammar points of academic English, useful vocabulary, and pronunciation skills that will improve your listening and speaking ability. There are no grammar, vocabulary, or pronunciation sections in the iBT, but you will need all these skills to do well in the reading, writing, listening, and speaking parts of the test.

Before you start studying *Step Up to the TOEFL® iBT for Intermediate Students*, look through a unit. You should see:

- the learning targets for the unit and how they are useful for the iBT
- examples of TOEFL®-level language in the grammar sections: don't worry if you can't understand these yet, but this is the type of language you will eventually read, hear, and use
- a list of **Words to Learn** from the chapter including common academic vocabulary from the Academic Word List
- **Step Up Notes** with useful hints and tips for the TOEFL® iBT itself.

Good luck as you prepare to take the next **step up** toward the TOEFL® iBT and your future studies!

# UNIT 1

# Chronology and Sequences

| Learning Targets | Importance on the iBT |
|---|---|
| Present tenses<br>—simple<br>—progressive<br>Past tenses<br>—simple<br>—progressive | • **iBT Reading and Listening:** recognize and understand these tenses to follow main ideas and supporting details<br>• **iBT Writing and Speaking:** control tenses for improved accuracy scores |
| Time signposts<br>Process signposts | • **iBT Writing and Speaking:** organize ideas using signposts<br>• **iBT Listening:** put the steps of a process in order; separate past from present events and states<br>• **iBT Reading:** insert sentences in a logical place; understand historical texts with dates, times, and sequences |
| Contractions<br>Endings with –ed | • **iBT Speaking:** use contractions and pronounce –ed endings correctly to improve the delivery score |

## Getting Started

*Discuss these questions with a partner or friend, or freewrite your answers. **Freewriting** means writing for a fixed time (for example, five minutes) without stopping. Don't worry about spelling, punctuation, or grammar. Just write your ideas in any order. This will improve your fluency and writing speed.*

1. What did you do last weekend? Say or write everything you can remember!

2. What are you thinking about right now? (Be honest!)

3. What do you usually do on a weekday morning?

Grammar You Can Use

## Simple Present and Present Progressive Tenses

The present tenses describe actions, feelings, and states that are **here and now.** Present tense verbs happen in the present, are true in the present, or are important in the present.

> "Herbal medicine **is** perhaps the fastest growing category of complementary and alternative medicine. Most patients **do not tell** their physicians about the use of dietary supplements, and relatively few physicians presently **inquire** about such use or are versed in herbal medicine."
>
> —*The Michigan Guide to English for Academic Success and Better TOEFL® Test Scores*, p. 35

Most academic writing is in the **simple present** tense. You will see this tense in iBT reading passages, and you should use it in the iBT writing section. Verbs in the simple present are **usually, generally,** or **always** true.

The **present progressive** is common in speaking, so you will hear it in conversations on the TOEFL® listening section. It describes the current situation. Verbs in the present progressive are true **right now** but could change soon. You can also use the present progressive in the independent speaking tasks to describe events that you think will happen soon (see also Unit 4).

| Simple Present | Present Progressive |
|---|---|
| I <u>am</u> a high-school student. | I <u>am thinking</u> about graduate school. |
| She <u>describes</u> problems with dormitories. | The problem <u>is growing</u>. |
| Story <u>is</u> not the same as plot. | <u>He's going</u> to the cafeteria. |
| Doctors <u>do</u> not <u>tell</u> their patients' secrets. | The professor <u>is</u> not <u>going</u> to stop. |

 *Watch Your Step!*

- When you're writing and speaking, remember the *-s* on simple present verbs that have third person *(he/she/it)* subjects (see Unit 7).
- In TOEFL® writing or speaking, do not use these verbs in the present progressive: *appear, seem, like, want, need, believe, know.* Because these words describe situations that are **always** or **generally** true and do not change, the simple present is better.
- A verb like *smell* (or *taste, think, consider,* etc.) can have one meaning in the simple present and a slightly different one in the present progressive. Compare *I think you are great* with *I am not thinking clearly.*
- See Appendix B for contractions that are used in conversation and informal writing.

## Exercise 1.1

*Underline the simple present verbs in these sentences. Circle the present progressive verbs. The first sentence has been done for you as an example.*

1. Meteorology <u>is</u> the study of weather. Forecasters (are getting) better at predicting the weather.

2. My favorite place is our basement. My band is using it to practice. When we're playing our music, my parents don't hear us!

3. Although English is the most widely spoken language in the U.S., the number of Spanish speakers is growing fast.

4. Today, we're talking about changes in beliefs about science. Are you all looking at page 125 in your textbook?

5. "I'm taking Econ 120 this semester, and I'm looking for the textbook. Where do you keep the Economics books?"

> **Step Up Note:** *On the iBT, you can only listen one time. However, for practice, you can listen more than once to the exercises in this book.*

**iBT**

## EXERCISE 1.2

Track 2. Listen to the conversation between two students about their study habits. Take notes as you listen. Use your notes to answer the questions. Choose the best answer.

1. What is the man doing?
   a. He's studying at the library.
   b. He's going to the coffee shop.
   c. He's going to the library.
   d. He's going to a biology class.

2. What is the woman doing?
   a. She's going to a coffee shop.
   b. She's going to the library.
   c. She's researching on the Internet.
   d. She's reading a book.

3. Where does the woman usually study?

   a.  in her dorm room

   b.  at the library

   c.  at the coffee shop

   d.  in a bookstore

**Step Up Note:** *You will usually see a question like Question 4 on the iBT.*

4. Track 3. Listen again to part of the conversation. Where does the man usually study?

   a.  in his dorm room

   b.  at the library

   c.  at the coffee shop

   d.  at the student union

5. Why is the man going to the library?

   a.  There's no Internet access at the coffee shop.

   b.  He's meeting his biology study group.

   c.  He doesn't like the taste of coffee.

   d.  He needs books for his research paper.

**Step Up Note:** *You could see similar questions on the iBT speaking test. You could also use some of the ideas in Exercise 1.3 in an independent writing task.*

## EXERCISE 1.3

Write a sentence to answer the questions. Use the correct tense (simple present or present progressive) in your sentence.

1. Where do you like to study?

   _____

2. Where are you studying today?

   _____

3. How do you usually go to school/work?

   _____

4. What are you doing later today?

   _____

5. What is happening in your town this week?

   _____

 Now, practice saying your sentences aloud.

## Simple Past and Past Progressive Tenses

The past tenses usually describe actions, states, and feelings that are **distant,** or not here and now. This usually means that they happened at a time in the past and are now finished. You will see past tenses in TOEFL® reading and listening passages when the speaker or writer wants to stress the past time of an event or make a contrast between the past and the present.

*Professor:* "Okay, we **were talking** about the Corn Belt . . . so I **went** through identifying the area and I **was talking** about the physical environment. Remember what I **talked** about in class? It **was** . . . "

—*The Michigan Guide to English for Academic Success and Better TOEFL® Test Scores,* p. 270

The **simple past** is quite common in listening, speaking, reading, and writing: it describes an action, state, or feeling that began and finished in the past.

The **past progressive** is less common in TOEFL® reading, but it is used in speaking, newspapers, and fiction. It often gives background descriptions for events that are described in the past simple.

| Simple Past | Past Progressive |
|---|---|
| I <u>was</u> excited about my birthday. | I <u>was eating</u> when you called. |
| She <u>studied</u> in the library. | In Europe, tensions <u>were growing</u>. |
| The war <u>was</u> not popular. | The plan <u>was</u> not <u>working</u>. |
| Video <u>did</u> not <u>kill</u> cinema. | I <u>was going</u> to call you, but my cell phone was broken. |

## Watch Your Step!

- Many common verbs have irregular simple past forms. It is very important to learn them! A list of the most useful verbs appears in Appendix A.
- See Appendix B for contractions that are used in conversation and informal writing.

## The Next Step

- The last past progressive example in the chart involves an action that you planned but did not do. The speaker planned to call, but it didn't happen because her phone was broken.

## Exercise 1.4

*Read the passage about Roanoke Island.*

---

When the first European explorers arrived in America, many people were already living there. They were the Native Americans, or American Indians. Christopher Columbus in 1492 was probably the first European to officially "discover" North America. After Columbus, there was a lot of trade between Europe and the Native Americans, but few Europeans moved to America. In 1587, more than 100 people from England started a village on Roanoke Island. Three years later, they were all dead. Perhaps while they were living on Roanoke Island, some Native Americans attacked and killed them. Today, many tourists visit Roanoke Island in North Carolina.

---

*Read the sentences about the passage.*

    a.  Perhaps Native Americans attacked the people on Roanoke Island.

    b.  Columbus "discovered" America in 1492.

    c.  Native Americans began living in North America.

    d.  Many tourists visit Roanoke Island.

    e.  There was a lot of trade between America and Europe.

    f.  In 1587, 100 people went from England to Roanoke Island.

    g.  All the English people died.

    h.  They lived on Roanoke Island for three years.

Complete the chart by putting Sentences a–h in the correct order of time (from the earliest event to the most recent):

1. _____

2. <u>Columbus "discovered" America in 1492.</u> _____

3. _____

4. _____

5. <u>They lived on Roanoke Island for three years.</u> _____

6. _____

7. _____

8. _____

---

***Step Up Note:*** *On the iBT integrated writing section, part of your task is to summarize what you heard.*

## EXERCISE 1.5

Track 4. Listen to the beginning of a class on American history.
Take notes as you listen. Write sentences summarizing this classroom discussion. Use the information in parentheses and your notes to help you. Choose the correct tense (simple past or past progressive). The first sentence has been done for you.

1. (when / finish last class / talk about Liberty Bell)

   <u>When the professor finished the last class, she was talking about the</u>

   <u>Liberty Bell.</u>

2. (professor / give quiz / but / wait until next week)

   _____

3. (Liberty Bell / gift from England)

   _____

4. (when / bell arrive in Philadelphia / crack appear)

_____

5. (another crack appear later / bell ring for Washington's birthday)

_____

6. (governor of Pennsylvania / try to create a free state)

_____

7. (people come to America / because / want freedom of religion)

_____

 Vocabulary You Need

## Time Signposts

A **signpost** is a phrase that a writer or speaker uses to point the reader or listener to the answer or to more understanding. Recognizing signposts can help you understand the organization of a TOEFL® reading or lecture. If you can use signposts correctly, your writing and speaking will be clear and easy to follow.

Time signposts tell you the order of events and also mark changes between the past and present. Study these common past and present time signposts:

| Specific Dates & Times | General Time Markers | Order of Events | Adjectives | Length of Time |
|---|---|---|---|---|
| at 8 AM | in the past | before | following | day |
| in 1587 | previously | after | previous | week |
| today | these days | during | next | month |
| on Monday | nowadays | while | last | year |
| in the spring | today | when | former | decade |
| (summer / | later | | | century |
| fall / autumn / | earlier | | | era |
| winter) | still | | | period |

 *Watch Your Step!*

- We say ***during*** *a conversation* but ***while*** *they were talking.*

## Exercise 1.6

*Choose the best word from the choices in parentheses to complete the sentences.* <u>Hint:</u> *Look at the **tense** of the verbs to help you decide.*

1. (Previously / Nowadays), the Internet was too expensive to install in most homes.

2. Louis XV became the king of France after the death of the (former / next) king, his father.

3. The 1960s was a (decade / century) of change in the United States.

4. (In / At) 1942, *Oklahoma!* began a record-breaking run on Broadway.

5. After a short (era / period) of time, the researcher measures the rat again.

**Step Up Note: Some of the reading passages on the iBT have a chart to complete.**

### EXERCISE 1.7

Read the passage about the history of musical theater. *Oklahoma!* is the name of a 1942 musical.

The musical *Oklahoma!* marked a turning point in the history of American musical theater. Before *Oklahoma!* musicals were collections of songs and dances without a real story. Sometimes, there was a song only for a star singer that did not fit the show. However, *Oklahoma!* was the first musical with a real story, like a play. The songs and dances helped to tell the story. Later musicals began to have more complicated stories. A new era in musical theater began, and musicals became a serious art form.

Place a check (✓) in the correct column in the chart to show the differences between musicals before and after *Oklahoma!*

|  | Before *Oklahoma!* | After *Oklahoma!* |
|---|---|---|
| 1. Collections of songs and dances |  |  |
| 2. No story |  |  |
| 3. A story like a play |  |  |
| 4. Songs and dances helped to tell the story |  |  |
| 5. More complicated stories |  |  |
| 6. A song for a star singer |  |  |
| 7. Musicals were a serious art form |  |  |

## Process Signposts

Processes are very important in all areas of academic language—the stages of change in history, the plot of novels and plays, the procedure for a science experiment, or instructions for an assignment. These process signposts help you recognize or explain the order of the stages of a process:

| The | first | stage  is . . . |
|-----|---------|-----------------|
|     | second  | step            |
|     | next    | point           |
|     | last    | procedure       |
|     | final   | part            |

Here are some other useful time signposts for describing a process:

| | |
|---|---|
| *Initially,* | *Immediately,* |
| *In the meantime / meanwhile,* | *Eventually,* |
| *At the same time,* | |

## Watch Your Step!

• Most of these words are **adverbs** (see Unit 5).

Finally, here are two useful verbs that talk about processes:

| | |
|---|---|
| *start out* = to begin | *arrive at* = end |

## Exercise 1.8

*Add process and time signposts to the paragraph. Do not use the same word twice!*

Most dramas follow a similar structure. The characters _____

by introducing themselves and their situation. In the next _____,

we learn about the major conflict, or problem. _____ , the

conflict builds to a climax. The minor characters are acting out smaller conflicts,

or sub-plots. These plots are resolved in the _____ stage of the

drama, called the "falling action." The _____ part is the

resolution, when the plot ends and all the characters _____ at a

satisfying conclusion.

## EXERCISE 1.9

Track 5. Listen to the lecture about immigrants' language patterns.
Take notes as you listen. Use your notes to answer the questions.
Choose the best answer.

1. What language did most first generation immigrants speak?

   a. English

   b. their first language

   c. both English and their first language

   d. Spanish

2. Which generation was bilingual?

   a. the first generation

   b. the second generation

   c. the third generation

   d. heritage language learners

3. How did this generation become bilingual, according to the lecture?

   a. They spoke only English at home and at school.

   b. They took special English as a Second Language classes.

   c. They spoke their parents' language at home; in the meantime, they learned English at school.

   d. They married native English speakers.

4. Track 6. Listen again to part of the lecture. What is a heritage language learner?

   a. a third-generation immigrant

   b. someone who has forgotten his or her parents' language

   c. someone who learns his or her ancestors' language and English at the same time

   d. someone who chooses to learn his or her ancestors' language after generations have passed

5. How does the professor organize the information he presents to the class?

   a. in the order that the language changes happen

   b. as a series of questions and answers

   c. going backward in time from the present

   d. in no particular order

## Words to Learn

Some common and useful words from Unit 1 follow. Words marked with an asterisk (*) are from the Academic Word List. The other words are very common in English or are useful for talking about education and universities.

| | | |
|---|---|---|
| academic* | experiment | research* |
| assignment* | freedom | state |
| character | generation* | student union |
| conversation | graduate | successful |
| crack | immigrant* | tourist |
| dormitory | native | village |
| drama* | predict* | weekday |
| economics* | | |

# Speaking Clearly

## Contractions

On the iBT listening section, you will notice that the speakers talk quite fast—probably faster than you! How do they do it? And how can you speak as quickly as a native speaker? One way is **contractions.** Contractions are reduced forms of verbs, especially in the present progressive, but also with some simple present verbs. A list of common contractions appears in Appendix B.

In a contraction, the verb becomes very short, and it can be hard to hear. Another word that is often replaced by a contraction is *not.* If you listen carefully for contractions, you will understand naturally spoken English better. If you use contractions, you will speak a little more fluently, and this will improve your delivery score on the TOEFL® speaking test.

### *Watch Your Step!*

- Don't use contractions in formal writing like the writing section of the iBT.

## Exercise 1.10

*Track 7. Listen to the sentences. Underline the verb that is replaced by a contraction, and write the shorter form (see Appendix B). The first one has been done for you as an example.*

1. I <u>am</u> looking for the admissions building. <u>I'm</u>_____

2. She is a great teacher! _____

3. You are joking! _____

4. Dr. Lin did not give any homework, did he? _____

5. Are you not going to the lab now? _____

6. I was not ready for the test. _____

7. We are on page 57. _____

8. The citizens are angry, and they are not afraid to fight. _____

*Now, practice reading the sentences with the contractions.*

## –ed Endings

The *–ed* ending on many simple past verbs and adjectives has three possible sounds, /t/ (e.g., *helped*), /d/ (e.g., *blamed*), or /ɪd/ (e.g., *interested*). Native speakers can be confused if you use the wrong sound.

## Exercise 1.11

*Track 8. Listen to the words, and write them in the correct column in the chart. The first three words have been done for you as examples.*

| helped | blamed | interested |
|--------|--------|------------|
| excited | looked | passed |
| wanted | shocked | allowed |
| received | watched | needed |

| /t/ | /d/ | /ɪd/ |
|-----|-----|------|
| helped | blamed | interested |
| | | |
| | | |
| | | |

**Step Up Note:** *This paragraph could be the answer to an iBT independent speaking question.*

### EXERCISE 1.12

Read the paragraph, and write in all the contractions above the verbs. Mark the correct pronunciation of all the *–ed* endings by writing /d/, /t/, or /ɪd/ above the words.

---

#### Describe a memory of a successful learning experience.

When I was a child, I played the piano. I was not very good, but I enjoyed the music. I am thinking now about one piece of music that I learned. I wanted to play it really well, but I needed more time. I practiced every day. Finally, in the concert, I managed to play the piece! My teacher said she was not surprised. She is a great piano player. She is always playing difficult music. But I was so excited.

---

Practice reading your answer aloud.

Track 9. Listen to the audio. Listen to the answer to the prompt. Check your answers. Try to speak the words in the paragraph along with the audio.

# UNIT 2

# Similarities and Differences

| Learning Targets | Importance on the iBT |
| --- | --- |
| Comparatives<br>Conjunctions | • **iBT Listening:** understand the organization of texts involving comparisons<br>• **iBT Reading:** recognize differences between ideas in the reading to learn questions; use conjunctions to understand the organization of passages<br>• **iBT Integrated Speaking and Writing:** contrast two opinions<br>• **iBT Writing:** use conjunctions (especially subordinating conjunctions) for a complex, academic style |
| Similarity signposts<br>Difference signposts | • **iBT Reading and Listening:** understand similarities and differences<br>• **iBT Writing and Speaking:** explain similarities and differences between things |
| Using stress to show contrast<br>Reduced vowels | • **iBT Listening, Integrated Writing and Speaking:** use stressed words to identify main ideas and answer questions; understand natural speech with many reduced vowels<br>• **iBT Speaking:** stress words and reduce vowels correctly to improve delivery |

## Getting Started

*Discuss these questions with a partner or friend, or freewrite your answers.*

1. How is your life different now from your life five years ago?

2. How are you similar to and different from your siblings or friends?

3. Which is more important for you: a job that pays you a lot of money or a very enjoyable job? Why?

## Grammar You Can Use

### Comparatives

Almost every substance contracts (takes up **less space**) as it gets **colder**. The same is true for water, until it reaches a temperature of 4 degrees Celsius. At that point, its volume increases until it gets **colder** . . .

—*The Michigan Guide to English for Academic Success and Better TOEFL® Test Scores*, p. 200

In the iBT listening and reading sections, many expressions of similarity or difference contain **comparative** structures. The most common comparatives are adjectives, but verbs, adverbs, and nouns also have comparative forms.

| Word | Greater Than (>) | Less Than (<) | The Same (=) | Not the Same (≠) |
|---|---|---|---|---|
| Short Adjective | *happier than* | *less happy than* | *as happy as* | *not as happy as* |
| Long Adjective | *more expensive than* | *less expensive than* | *as expensive as* | *not as expensive as* |
| Adverb | *more quickly than* | *less quickly than* | *as quickly as* | *not as quickly as* |
| Verb | *eats more than* | *eats less than* | *eats as much as* | *does not eat as much as* |
| Count Noun | *more trees than* | *fewer trees than* | *as many trees as* | *not as many trees as* |
| Non-Count Noun | *more water than* | *less water than* | *as much water as* | *not as much water as* |

 ### Watch Your Step!

- Most short adjectives (one syllable, sometimes two) form the comparative by adding *–er*.
- Most long adjectives (more than two syllables, sometimes two) form the comparative with *more* or *less*.
- The best way to learn which comparative form a two-syllable adjective takes is by paying attention to these forms in your reading and listening. Eventually, the correct form will simply look or sound right to you.
- Don't add *–er* to *–ly* adverbs (not *\*quicklier*) or nouns.
- Count nouns have a plural form (*trees*); non-count nouns are not usually plural (not *\*waters*).

## Exercise 2.1

*Add a comparative form to the sentences using the information in parentheses. The first one has been done for you as an example.*

1. *(> tall)* The Sears Tower is <u>taller than</u> the Hancock Tower.

2. *(< interesting)* The details of Shakespeare's life are _____ his plays.

3. *(= dangerous)* Not wearing a seatbelt is _____ not wearing a helmet when riding a bicycle.

4. *(> slowly)* Most people write _____ they speak.

5. *(< choices)* If you don't take your required classes this year, you will have _____ next year.

6. *(≠ consume)* People in Africa _____ Americans.

## EXERCISE 2.2

Track 10. Listen to the lecture about photography.
Take notes as you listen. Complete the chart with information from the lecture.
You will not use two of the answer choices.

| Film cameras | 1. |
| | 2. |
| Digital cameras | 1. |
| | 2. |
| | 3. |

a. newer
b. more professional photographers
c. less popular for amateurs
d. easier to use
e. fewer mistakes
f. harder to edit
g. more expensive

## EXERCISE 2.3

Write two sentences comparing each of the items. Remember that a comparison can show a similarity or a difference and that you can compare more than two things. The first two sentences have been done for you as examples.

1. watching a movie in the theater / watching a movie on DVD / watching a movie on TV

   *Watching a movie in the theater is more exciting than watching a movie on DVD or on TV.*

   *Watching a movie on DVD or TV is cheaper than watching a movie in the theater.*

2. dorm (dormitory) / apartment

   _____

   _____

3. airplanes / trains / cars

   _____

   _____

4. high school graduates / college graduates

   _____

   _____

5. life in the 1800s / life today

   _____

   _____

# Conjunctions

A **conjunction** is a word that joins two clauses into one sentence. A **clause** is a group of words with at least a subject and a verb. There are two types of conjunctions, and it is important to understand the difference between them to avoid mistakes on the iBT writing section.

The seven **coordinating conjunctions** *(for, and, nor, but, or, yet, so)* connect two ideas that are each as important as the other. **Subordinating conjunctions** (e.g., *while, when, although, because, since, as, whereas*) connect a main idea to a less important idea such as a reason, cause, explanation, time, or condition.

**Although** it is tempting today to consider the Michigan that became a territory in 1805 an unaltered Eden, it had in fact been home to generations of people since the end of the last glaciations approximately 10,000 years ago.

—*The Michigan Guide to English for Academic Success and Better TOEFL® Test Scores*, p. 63

---

**Coordinating Conjunctions**

You can take Math 101 this semester |, and| you can take Math 102 in the spring.

The library is open all night |, but| the computer lab closes at 10 PM.

Henry VIII wanted a divorce |, or| he was going to leave the Catholic church.

Hybrid cars use less gasoline |, so| they are better for the environment.

**Subordinating Conjunctions**

Newton was an important scientist |because| he described gravity.

|Because| he described gravity |,| Newton was an important scientist.

Physics and chemistry are physical sciences |whereas| psychology and economics are social sciences.

|Whereas| psychology and economics are social sciences |,| physics and chemistry are physical sciences.

---

### Watch Your Step!

- Note the different use of commas with coordinating and subordinating conjunctions.
- Do not start sentences with coordinating conjunctions in academic writing (e.g., the writing section of the iBT). This is bad style in formal writing.

*The Next Step*

- *For* is similar to *because,* but we do not use it often. *Yet* is a stronger form of *but;* it is not common, but you might see it in academic reading.
- Use a variety of conjunctions in your iBT writing responses. In academic writing tasks like these, native speakers use many **subordinating conjunctions.**

 **Exercise 2.4**

*Join the sentences with the conjunction in parentheses to make one new sentence. Pay attention to the commas! The first one has been done for you as an example.*

1.  Babies can recognize any human sound.

    They can learn any language. *(and)*

    <u>Babies can recognize any human sound, and they can learn any language.</u>

2.  Coal and diamonds have the same atoms.

    They have different structures. *(but)*

    _____

    _____

3.  Some musicals are sung without any speaking.

    They are similar to operas. *(so)*

    _____

    _____

4.  A volt is a unit of electricity.

    A joule is a unit of energy. *(whereas)*

    _____

    _____

5.  Humans have used language for thousands of years.

    Writing is a more recent invention. *(although)*

    _____

    _____

## EXERCISE 2.5

Read the paragraph about the planet Mars.

In many ways, Mars is similar to Earth, but people cannot live on Mars. Although Mars has a red color, it is not hot. Mars is further from the Sun than the Earth, so it is colder than Earth, and the temperature on Mars changes more than on Earth. There is less water in the atmosphere of Mars than in Earth's atmosphere, and there is probably no water on the surface. Whereas people can breathe on Earth, they cannot breathe on Mars.

Complete the chart to show the differences between Earth and Mars. Two of the answer choices will not be used.

| Mars | 1. |
| | 2. |
| | 3. |
| Earth | 1. |
| | 2. |

a. less oxygen in the atmosphere
b. warmer
c. further from the Sun
d. more water in atmosphere
e. higher mountains
f. no water on surface
g. people cannot breathe

Vocabulary You Need

## Similarity Signposts

You have already seen two grammatical ways to make comparisons in this unit. There are also vocabulary signposts for similarities and differences. You will see these in the reading and listening sections of the iBT. Study these words and phrases, which are signposts for **similarity**.

---

**Adjectives and adverbs that show similarities:**

**similar to** (adjective/preposition). *Softball is similar to baseball.*
Remember that *similar to* doesn't mean "the same as."
**alike** (adjective / adverb).    *The violin and the viola look alike, but they sound*
                                   *different.*
                                   *Violence is a problem for teenagers and adults alike.*
*Alike* never goes in front of a noun. As an adverb, it usually goes at the end of a sentence. It means "similar" or "equally."

---

**Verbs that show similarities:**

**resemble** (verb). *At night, the city resembles a ghost town.*
*Resemble* means "look like." It sometimes is used to give an example from a different field (a metaphor).
**share** (verb). *Photography and cinema share many techniques.*
Here, *share* means that things or people have something in common.

---

**Phrases that show similarities:**

**have something in common (with).** *All acids have one thing in common.*
                                     *One problem the governments have in common*
                                     *is poverty.*
                                     *Camus' philosophy has a lot in common with*
                                     *Sartre's.*
*In common* means that two things have the same feature or characteristic.
**both ... and ...**          *Both eye color and hair color are decided by your genes.*
**not only ... (but) also ...**    *The Internet not only changed our communication style,*
                                   *but it also influenced the English language.*
The *not only* part of the sentence usually refers to an idea described earlier. *But also* introduces a new topic or surprising information.

*Step Up Note: The iBT listening section sometimes asks you to categorize information or complete a chart like this one.*

## EXERCISE 2.6

Track 11. Listen to the first part of the lecture about two cultures.
Take notes as you listen. Place a check (✓) in the correct column in the chart to reflect the information in the lecture.

|  | True | False |
|---|---|---|
| 1. The Ancient Greeks and Romans shared similar religions. |  |  |
| 2. Both Greeks and Romans believed there was one god. |  |  |
| 3. The arts were important for Greeks and Romans alike. |  |  |
| 4. The Greeks and Romans shared ideas about government. |  |  |
| 5. The Greeks and Romans had kings in common. |  |  |

## Difference Signposts

English words often live in families. A **word family** is a group of related words with different uses. Most word families have a mixture of nouns, verbs, adjectives, and adverbs. Some word families occur frequently in academic writing such as on the iBT listening and reading sections, and you should use them in the writing and speaking sections. Study these academic word families that signpost differences:

### The *different* word family:

**different from/than** (adj). *The second theory is very different from the first.*
**difference between** (noun). *There are many differences between radar and sonar.*
Be careful to use the correct form!
**differ in** (verb). *Cultures differ in their values.*
**differ from** (verb). *German grammar differs from English in word order.*
*Differ in* tells you the kind of difference; *differ from* tells you the two things that are different.

**The *contrast* word family:**

**contrast** (noun). *Notice the contrast between these two businesses.*
**contrast with** (verb). *Austen's style contrasts with Bronte's.*
A contrast is a very clear difference.
**contrasting** (adj). *Büchner wrote two contrasting short plays on the same theme.*
**in contrast to** (phrase). *The Ojibwe cooperated with the European traders in contrast to the Sioux, who fought against the newcomers.*

**Other words to signpost difference:**

**unlike** (adj/prep). *Costa Rica is unlike most countries because it has no army.*
*Unlike the meat-eating tyrannosaurus rex, the brontosaurus was a vegetarian.*
**distinction** (noun). *Chemists make a distinction between organic and inorganic matter.*
Notice the verb *make* is often used with *distinction* in this meaning.
**opposite** (adj). *A base is the opposite of an acid.*
Two opposites have entirely different properties. Although acids and bases are both chemical compounds, they behave in different ways.

### EXERCISE 2.7

Track 12. Listen to the second part of the lecture about Greece and Rome. Take notes as you listen. Place a check (✓) in the correct column in the chart to reflect the information in the lecture.

| | Greece | Rome |
|---|---|---|
| 1. Every citizen voted for every decision (democracy). | | |
| 2. The emperor made many decisions. | | |
| 3. The god of war was called Mars. | | |
| 4. The emperor was more powerful. | | |
| 5. They kept their old religion. | | |

## Exercise 2.8

*Choose two books, movies, or plays that you know well. Describe how they are similar and different. Write five sentences using different words from the lists of signposts on pages 22–24. Discuss your ideas with a partner or friend.*

_____

_____

_____

_____

_____

_____

_____

_____

_____

_____

_____

## Words to Learn

Some common and useful words from Unit 2 follow. Words marked with an asterisk (*) are from the Academic Word List.

| | | |
|---|---|---|
| activity | digital | semester |
| ancient | gene | social sciences |
| chemical* | influenced | surface |
| citizen | nature | technique* |
| consume* | nurture | theory* |
| cooperate* | poverty | values |
| culture* | powerful | violence |
| democracy | salary | |

Speaking Clearly

## Using Stress to Show Contrast

A word or syllable has **stress** when it is louder, slower, and a little higher than the other words or syllables near it. Sometimes, we use stress to signpost a contrast. We do this by stressing the two things that are different. For example, in this sentence, the stressed syllables are underlined:

*I agree with your <u>first</u> point, but I don't agree with your <u>second</u> point.*

The speaker is making a contrast between the first and second points.

If you understand stress in lectures and conversations, you will be better able to answer some of the organization and pragmatics questions on the iBT listening. If you use stress correctly on the iBT speaking tasks, you will be able to communicate your opinion more effectively.

 **Exercise 2.9**

 *Track 13. Listen to the sentences. Underline the stressed words. The first one has been done for you as an example.*

1. <u>Trains</u> are <u>fast</u>, but <u>airplanes</u> are <u>faster</u>.

2. Astronomy is the study of the stars, while astrology means predicting the future.

3. Unlike basketball, hockey is not a popular TV sport.

4. I'm interested in the class, but I don't like the professor.

5. So, you're saying that protons have a positive charge, and electrons have a negative charge?

### EXERCISE 2.10

1. Read the paragraph. Underline the words that have stress to signpost contrast.

#### What are the differences between universities and community colleges?

Most people go to a university for four years, but you go to a community college for two years. Universities are also very expensive, but community colleges are cheaper. Also, you can be in a large class at a university, but a small class at a community college. Universities are mostly academic, unlike community colleges, which are often vocational.*

2. Track 14. Listen to the audio. Listen to the answer to the prompt. Check your answers.

3. Read the passage with the audio. Make sure that you put stress in the right places.

## Reduced Vowels

When you listen to native speakers of English and compare their speech to written words, you can see that they don't pronounce every vowel the same way. When a vowel does not have stress, it is usually reduced to a short, fast, low sound called the *schwa*, or /ə/.

If you can reduce vowels in the right places, you will be able to speak faster and more naturally. This will improve your iBT speaking score. Recognizing spoken words with vowel reductions is essential to your success in the listening section of the iBT. You can hear reduced vowels in almost all fluent spoken English.

---

* Vocational classes teach you how to do a job.

## Exercise 2.11

*Read the two lists of words, and then listen to Track 15 on the audio. In the first list, all the reduced vowels have been crossed out and replaced with a schwa symbol /ə/.*

| ə<br>LIST 1. a. pizzə | ə<br>b. college | ə<br>c. teacher | ə<br>d. vowel | ə  ə<br>e. similar |
|---|---|---|---|---|
| LIST 2. a. water | b. unit | c. different | d. listen | e. resemble |

Listen to the audio again (Track 15), and repeat each word. Then, cross out the reduced syllables in List 2 and replace them with schwas.
Practice saying each word aloud.

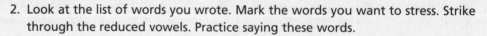

*Step Up Note: This is an independent speaking prompt that is similar to one you might see on the iBT.*

## EXERCISE 2.12

### Describe a teacher who was very important to you.
### Explain why this teacher was important.

1. In the space provided, make notes to help you answer the question. Don't write complete sentences. Write the key words you will need.

_____

_____

_____

_____

2. Look at the list of words you wrote. Mark the words you want to stress. Strike through the reduced vowels. Practice saying these words.

3. Now, speak your answer. On the iBT test, you will have 45 seconds to answer a question like this, but for practice you can speak longer if you want to. If possible, record your voice on a cassette or computer.

4. Listen to your answer, or ask a friend or teacher to listen to it. Answer these questions.

   a. Did you stress important and contrasting words?

   b. Did you reduce some of the unstressed vowels?

   c. Did your speech sound fluent and connected?

# Developing Ideas

| Learning Targets | Importance on the iBT |
|---|---|
| Pronouns<br>Sentence connectors | • **iBT Reading:** answer questions about pronoun reference<br>• **iBT Speaking and Writing:** use connecting words and pronouns to improve organization and development scores |
| Development signposts<br>Synonyms | • **iBT Listening:** find the main ideas of a passage and understand the relationship between them; recognize the difference between a continuing idea and a new topic<br>• **iBT Reading:** locate all the main ideas and distinguish between main and supporting ideas; understand unknown words by using context and synonyms<br>• **iBT Writing and Speaking:** use synonyms to show a range of vocabulary; develop ideas and paragraphs in an academic style |
| Thought groups<br>Major stress | • **iBT Speaking:** improve fluency with thought groups and correct stress |

## Getting Started

*Discuss these questions with a partner or friend, or freewrite your answers.*

1. Who are the other members of your family? Describe them.

2. Can you describe an idea that you learned in a recent class? Give as much detail as you can.

Grammar You Can Use

## Pronouns

**Pronouns** are small words that can replace nouns. Pronouns connect ideas without repeating a noun many times, which is not good style. When you meet a pronoun in the TOEFL® reading or listening sections, it is very important to find its referent. The **referent** is the noun which the pronoun replaces. You should also use pronouns in TOEFL® speaking and writing, but always make sure that there is a clear referent. A complete list of pronouns is in Appendix C.

> "The chemical composition of ink is one indicator of authenticity in a map or drawing, but **it** is not the only one. **It** is certainly not dependable enough to be the sole factor in deciding whether a work is genuine or a forgery."
>
> —*The Michigan Guide to English for Academic Success and Better TOEFL® Test Scores*, p. 7

Students can live on campus, or *they* can live away from *it.*

 *Watch Your Step!*

- Note the correct spelling of *its* (not *it's*) and *their.*
- The pronoun for any singular, non-human noun is *it: I enjoyed **the book.** It asked many interesting questions.*
- The pronoun for all plural nouns is *they: Trains are comfortable, but they are not reliable.*
- It is polite to put yourself second: *My wife and I* not *I and my wife.*

 *The Next Step*

- Most pronouns refer back to a noun or noun phrase; for example, *he* usually refers back to the last male, human noun. However, if a sentence starts with a dependent clause, the pronoun could refer forward (e.g., *Because **it** can cause birth defects, pregnant women should not drink **alcohol.***

## Exercise 3.1

*Underline all the pronouns in the sentences, and draw arrows between each pronoun and its referent. Some sentences have two or more pronouns. The first one has been done for you as an example.*

1. Sound travels in waves. <u>Their</u> length varies according to the pitch of the sound.

2. Children are born with the ability to speak any language, but they only actually learn the language of their environment.

3. Darwin began to think about evolution on his voyage to the Galapagos Islands.

4. The Americans with Disabilities Act guarantees disabled people their basic human rights.

5. Although they are not accepted by many Western doctors, some herbs are often used as medications in the East.

## Exercise 3.2

*Fill the blanks with the correct pronoun. Tip: Think about the noun that the pronoun replaces. The first one has been done for you as an example.*

1. Many modern novels try to confuse *their* readers.

2. All students should take a foreign language class. _____ will learn to understand other cultures.

3. I'd like to take Professor Wein's class. _____ is a really good teacher. *[Professor Wein is a man.]*

4. CDs replaced audiocassettes because _____ sound quality was much better.

5. I don't like my advisor. I don't think that she listens to _____.

6. Cherokee is a dying language because few children are learning to speak _____.

## EXERCISE 3.3

Read the paragraph about the history of tea. Then, answer the questions about the pronouns.

## Tea

The British drink an average of three cups of tea a day, and they have been drinking it for more than 350 years. However, the tradition of drinking tea came from China, and tea has been its national drink for more than a thousand years. The Chinese tell a story about the origins of tea, although it is probably not entirely true. The Emperor Shen Nung was boiling water outside one day. Suddenly, some leaves from a tea bush blew into his pot of water. They brewed into the first pot of tea.

1. The British drink an average of three cups of tea a day, and <u>they</u> have been drinking <u>it</u> for more than 350 years. The word *they* in this sentence refers to:
   a. the British
   b. cups
   c. tea
   d. years

2. In the same sentence, the word *it* refers to:
   a. the British
   b. cups
   c. tea
   d. day

3. However, the tradition of drinking tea came from China, and tea has been <u>its</u> national drink for more than a thousand years. The word *its* in this sentence refers to:
   a. tradition
   b. tea
   c. China
   d. drink

4. The Chinese tell a story about the origins of tea, although <u>it</u> is probably not entirely true. The word *it* in this sentence refers to:

a. Chinese

b. story

c. China

d. tea

5. The Emperor Shen Nung was boiling water outside one day. Suddenly, some leaves from a tea bush blew into <u>his</u> pot of water. The word *his* in the second sentence refers to:

a. the Emperor Shen Nung

b. water

c. day

d. bush

6. <u>They</u> brewed into the first pot of tea. The word *they* in this sentence refers to:

a. the Emperor Shen Nung

b. water

c. leaves

d. tea bush

## Sentence Connectors

In Unit 2, you learned about two ways to connect ideas into one sentence: **coordinating** and **subordinating conjunctions.** There is another group of connecting words and phrases that show the development of an idea. These words and phrases are called **sentence connectors** because they connect the ideas between two sentences.

Understanding sentence connectors in the TOEFL® reading and listening sections will help you recognize the relationship between ideas. Using sentence connectors improves your cohesion and development in speaking and writing.

"The most important languages in the world, and the ones that we should be focusing our attention on, are languages that are dying. **For example,** Navajo is a Native American language that is dying as Navajo children learn English in order to be successful in the larger U.S. economy and culture. **As a result,** many Navajo children lose their Navajo, causing the language to slowly die."

—*The Michigan Guide to English for Academic Success and Better TOEFL® Test Scores*, p. 135

| Function | Sentence Connectors | Examples |
|---|---|---|
| Continuing idea *(and)* | *also*<br>*additionally*<br>*in addition*<br>*furthermore* | Children learn language from their parents. *In addition,* they learn academic language at school. They *also* learn slang from their peers. |
| Contrast or opposite idea *(but)* | *however*<br>*in contrast*<br>*on the other hand* | Cheese contains important proteins. *However,* it is also high in fat. |
| Result *(so)* | *therefore*<br>*as a result*<br>*consequently* | The U.S. economy crashed in 1929. *As a result,* unemployment rose sharply. |
| Example | *for example*<br>*for instance* | The higher cost of oil affects people in many ways. *For example,* airline tickets are more expensive. |

## Watch Your Step!

- Most sentence connectors can appear at the beginning, in the middle, or at the end of sentences. However, they are most common at the beginning of sentences in academic writing.
- *Also* is most common in the middle of sentences in academic writing. It usually comes after the subject. *Also* is not used at the end of sentences in good writing.
- Take care with the punctuation. Do <u>not</u> join two sentences with a comma and a sentence connector (not \**Children learn language from their parents, in addition, they learn slang from their peers.*). <u>Do</u> put a comma after a sentence connector at the start of a sentence (*Children learn language from their parents. **In addition,** they learn slang from their peers.*).

## Exercise 3.4

*Add a sentence connector to the sentences, and punctuate correctly. The first one has been done for you as an example.*

1. Twins usually spend a lot of time together. <u>As a result</u>, they can communicate in special ways.

2. The conductor helps the orchestra keep time _____ he or she decides the mood and interpretation of the music.

3. Some bacteria cause illnesses in the human body _____ other types of bacteria are important for health.

4. The Great Lakes are a valuable source of fish _____ they are an essential means of transportation.

5. Chimpanzees can produce some kinds of language _____ they cannot produce the same range of expression as humans.

**Step Up Note:** *Not all the listenings on the iBT are lectures. You will also hear discussions about life at a North American university.*

## EXERCISE 3.5

Track 16. Listen to the conversation during a professor's office hours about the requirements for a linguistics class.

Take notes as you listen. Place a check (✓) in the correct column in the table to reflect what the student can and cannot use to write her research paper.

|  | Use | Don't Use |
|---|---|---|
| 1. Library books |  |  |
| 2. Field data |  |  |
| 3. Tape recording |  |  |
| 4. Internet sources |  |  |

**Step Up Note:** *The ideas in Exercise 3.6 could answer an iBT independent writing prompt.*

## EXERCISE 3.6

### Agree or disagree with the following statement:
### Parents are the best teachers.

Write sentences using the ideas given. Add sentence connectors, and punctuate correctly. The first one has been done for you as an example.

1. babies' first contact is with their parents / they learn to smile by copying their parents / children learn social behavior from them.

   *Babies' first contact is with their parents. For example, they learn to smile by copying their parents. As a result, children learn social behavior from them.*

2. some parents are not kind to their children / these parents are not the best teachers / children need other teachers

   _____

   _____

3. children learn good behavior from their parents / they learn bad behavior / sometimes parents argue in front of their children / these children do not grow up to be polite

   _____

   _____

   _____

4. parents can teach their children a lot / young people learn more from their friends / they learn how to play on a team / they learn how to resolve an argument

   _____

   _____

   _____

Vocabulary You Need

## Development Signposts

In most academic writing and speaking, ideas are developed over several sentences or even paragraphs. To help you follow ideas and recognize new topics on the iBT reading and listening tests, writers and speakers often use **development signposts.** These signposts point you toward the development of an idea.

There are two groups of development signposts. **Continuing idea signposts** point you ahead in the next step of the same idea. Two important continuing idea signposts are the special pronouns *this* (singular) and *these* (plural). You sometimes see a **general noun** after *this* or *these* (e.g., *idea, situation, changes*). On the other hand, **new idea signposts** tell you that the writer or speaker has finished one idea and is starting a new point.

| Continuing Idea Signposts | New Idea Signposts |
|---|---|
| *This idea* | *Another reason* |
| *This argument* | *The other problem* |
| *This situation* | *The second development* |
| *This change* | *A further problem* |
| *This discovery* | |

 *Watch Your Step!*

- When you **read** a continuing idea signpost, always look **back** in the text for the referent.
- When you **hear** a continuing idea signpost, draw an arrow (→) in your notes to help you see the connection between the ideas.
- New idea signposts help you keep ideas separate in your notes or help you understand the structure of a reading passage.
- Note that *another* is one word; it means you are giving the next point in a series of many points. *The other* is two words and it means you are giving the second of two points.

## Exercise 3.7

*Circle the development signposts in the paragraph about culture shock. Draw arrows from **continuing** idea signposts to the ideas that they continue. Write a slash (/) in the text when you see a **new idea** signpost. The first signpost has been marked for you as an example.*

Culture shock is the uncomfortable feeling you have when you live for a time in a different country. This feeling is normal, but you can reduce the effects of culture shock. These actions sound simple, but they are very effective. The first thing you can do is keep contact with friends and family at home. Another idea is to join a club, society, or religious organization. This will give you some support in the new country. A further solution is physical exercise. Some people find this very helpful when they are frustrated.

> **Step Up Note:** *In the iBT integrated writing task, you have to connect ideas between a listening passage and a written text.*

## EXERCISE 3.8

Use the words in the box to fill the blanks. Do not use any word more than once. Each blank begins a sentence that either continues the last idea or starts a new topic. The first one has been done for you as an example.

| another | decrease | improvement | reason |
|---------|----------|-------------|--------|
| change  | idea     | other       | this   |

1. Fewer people are buying newspapers today. This _decrease._ . . .

2. Vitamin C may protect you from sickness. This _____. . . .

3. Burning coal causes a lot of pollution. _____ disadvantage. . .

4. As the ice caps melt, ocean levels rise. _____ means. . . .

5. Many serious diseases from the past can now be prevented. This _____. . . .

## Synonyms

Synonyms are words with very similar meanings. You can replace a word with its synonym and the sentence will still be true. The authors and speakers on the TOEFL® test use synonyms because it is not usually good style to repeat the same word many times.

Synonyms also create connections between your ideas in the writing and speaking tasks without using connecting words. Good writers sometimes prefer not to use a lot of sentence connectors.

### Exercise 3.9

*Read the words in the box. Then, rewrite them in the correct circle of connected words. They are not all close synonyms, but all the words in each circle should express a similar idea.*

| | | | | |
|---|---|---|---|---|
| academic | decline | grow | ~~lesson~~ | reduce |
| advance | development | idea | problem | rise |
| challenge | go down | improvement | project | seminar |
| college | go up | issue | proposal | university |
| course | | | | |

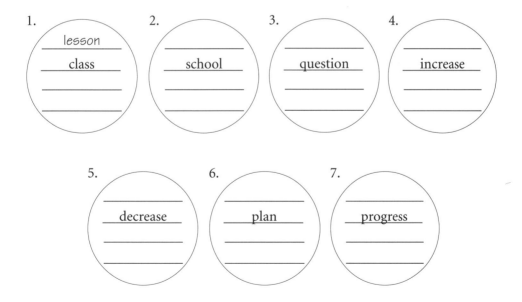

1. lesson / class
2. school
3. question
4. increase
5. decrease
6. plan
7. progress

> **Step Up Note:** *Some of the questions on the reading section of the iBT ask you to explain the meaning of new or technical words. You can do this if you use the clues in the text.*

## EXERCISE 3.10

Read the paragraph about nutrition.

---

Americans are eating more and more sugar. As a result, the population is getting fatter. The average U.S. adult eats 2½ pounds of sugar a week. Sugary products are everywhere, and it is genuinely hard for |people| to avoid |saccharides|. Among children, |this problem| is even worse. Kids see advertisements for candy on TV, in newspapers, and in magazines. However, they don't see the dangers of eating too many sweets in the |media|. Consequently, too many young people are overweight, and |obesity| can lead to other serious health problems in later life.

---

1. Who are the *people* referred to in the fourth sentence?
   a. all people in the world
   b. American children
   c. the average U.S. adult
   d. the American population

2. What does the word *saccharides* mean? (<u>Tip</u>: Don't use a dictionary! Find a synonym in the text.)
   a. Americans
   b. population
   c. sugar
   d. advertisements

3. What is *this problem* in the fifth sentence?
   a. The American population is getting fatter.
   b. The average American eats 2½ pounds of sugar a week.
   c. Sugary products are everywhere.
   d. It is hard for people to avoid saccharides.

4. What does the word *media* mean in this passage? (<u>Tip</u>: Again, use the signposts in the text.)

   a. sugary products

   b. TV, newspapers, and magazines

   c. young people

   d. movies

5. What does the word *obesity* mean? (<u>Tip</u>: You're looking for a synonym in the text.)

   a. being overweight

   b. eating too many sweets

   c. watching too much television

   d. being sick

## Words to Learn

Some common and useful words from Unit 3 follow. Words marked with an asterisk (*) are from the Academic Word List.

| | | |
|---|---|---|
| ability | data* | relationship |
| advisor | increase | reliable* |
| affect* | interpretation* | requirement* |
| argue, argument | media* | resolve* |
| average | obesity | unemployment |
| behavior | population | valuable |
| campus | prevent | vary* |

 Speaking Clearly

## Thought Groups

In writing, a sentence is a complete idea; you can recognize a sentence because it starts with a capital letter and ends with a period, question mark, or exclamation point. When we join sentences with conjunctions or other grammar structures, it is usually easy to see the different ideas in the sentences. Spoken English, which you will hear on the TOEFL® listening passages, is different because the listener can't see the words or hear most punctuation marks. Therefore, speakers use **thought groups** to help the listener identify the main ideas and to know when to pause.

A thought group is a complete thought. It might be the same as a written sentence, but it is not always. Native speakers try not to pause during a thought group. If the idea (or sentence) is not finished, the thought group ends with **rising intonation** (your voice goes up a little). If the idea (or sentence) is finished, the thought group ends with **falling intonation** (your voice goes down a little). Using thought groups correctly on the iBT speaking test will help the listener follow the development of your ideas.

### Exercise 3.11

*Track 17. Listen to the introduction to a lecture about English theater in the 16th century. Note that the speaker has a British accent.*

1. Read the lecture as you listen again to Track 17. Mark the end of each thought group with a slash (/). The first / has been entered for you as an example.

   In today's lecture / I'm going to talk about English theater in the late 16th century. The most famous writer, of course, was William Shakespeare, but he had a lot of competition. The most popular play of the 1580s, for example, was called *The Spanish Tragedy,* by Thomas Kyd. We don't know exactly when it was performed, but it was probably first acted in London in the 1580s.

2. Listen again, and mark in the rising intonation ( ) and falling intonation ( ). The first two intonation marks have been made for you as examples.

3. Read the paragraph with the lecturer, matching his intonation and thought groups. Since the speaker has a British accent, some of his pronunciation is different from American English. However, the thought groups are the same.

*Step Up Note: The questions in Exercise 3.12 are similar to those on the independent speaking section of the iBT.*

## EXERCISE 3.12

Talk for a minute on each of the questions. If you are working with a partner, listen for your partner's intonation, and say if the thought groups are clear. Otherwise, record your answers. Listen to your answers, and ask yourself if your thought groups are clear.

1. Describe a book, play, or film that you like. Why do you like it?

2. What is your favorite school subject, or what subject do you want to study at university? Why do you like it?

3. Describe a very happy or unhappy day. Why was it happy or unhappy?

## Major Stress

On the iBT listening section, you will hear that some words get more stress than others. When a word has stress, it is a little louder, higher, and slower than the other words (see Unit 2). In general, each thought group has one word with the **major stress.** If you stress every word in a thought group on the iBT speaking test, it might be hard to understand your ideas, and you will speak too slowly.

### The word with the major stress is generally:

1. the *last* **content word** in the thought group (a content word is a noun, verb, adjective, or adverb, but not small words like *the, a, an, of, it, is,* etc.); OR

2. the content word that gives **new or surprising information.**

For example, *I prefer to <u>work</u> / in the <u>library</u>. The library is <u>quiet</u> / and it's <u>open</u> / all <u>night</u>.*

## Exercise 3.13

*Read the conversation between a student and his advisor. Mark a slash (/) where you expect a thought group to end. Underline the words you expect to have the major stress.*

*Student:*  I have a question about my classes.

*Advisor:*  What's your major?

*Student:*  I'm a business major, but I have to take a writing class.

*Advisor:*  Everyone has to do that!

*Student:*  I understand. I'm interested in history, so I want to take a history composition class.

*Advisor:*  That's possible. Next semester, there's a class on American history.

*Student:*  But the class is full!

*Advisor:*  Let me call the department. If you're lucky, they'll say yes.

Track 18. Listen to the conversation. Check your answers.

# UNIT 4

# Cause, Effect, and Correlation

| Learning Targets | Importance on the iBT |
|---|---|
| Present perfect tense Talking about the future | • **iBT Reading and Listening:** understand the relationship between ideas; recognize changes between the past, present, and future; distinguish cause and correlation<br>• **iBT Writing and Speaking:** talk about the past, present, and future; describe changes, for example, in your life |
| Cause-and-effect signposts Cause or correlation? | • **iBT Reading:** answer information and inference questions<br>• **iBT Listening:** understand organization and connecting content questions<br>• **iBT Integrated Writing and Speaking:** describe connections between ideas<br>• **iBT Independent Writing and Speaking:** make predictions, analyze situations for causes, effects, and correlations |
| Reductions Linking | • **iBT Listening:** understand natural speech in conversations and lectures; recognize linked words<br>• **iBT Speaking:** use different levels of language; make speech more natural by reducing some verbs and linking some sounds |

## Getting Started

*Discuss these questions with a partner or friend, or freewrite your answers.*

1. Why are you studying English?

2. Why do you want to take the TOEFL® iBT?

3. Talk or write about a big decision you made. How did you make the decision? What happened as a result of your decision?

# Grammar You Can Use

## Present Perfect Tense

> "The DSHEA **has had** enormous popular appeal yet **has generated** controversy among regulatory authorities. Since the statute's enactment, various regulatory proposals **have circulated** to further restrict consumer access to dietary supplements."
>
> —*The Michigan Guide to English for Academic Success and Better TOEFL® Test Scores*, p. 69

The **present perfect** is a present tense, but it is used to look back at the past from the present. As a result, it is *not* used to talk about specific, completed events at a particular time. Instead, the present perfect is used to talk about things that happened **before now;** we are not interested in exactly *when* the event happened. The present perfect often describes a change— something has happened until now, or has changed in recent years.

You will often hear or read the present perfect in the introductions to texts or topics on the iBT. The present perfect is common in academic writing, so you need to use it in the iBT writing tasks.

| Subject | Present Tense of *Have* | Past Participle |
|---|---|---|
| I | have | been to the Grand Canyon. |
| The population | has | increased. |

## Watch Your Step!

- Some verbs have irregular past participles. A list of the most common irregular verbs is in Appendix A. You need to learn these forms.
- Don't forget to use *has* for he/she/it/singular nouns (see Unit 7).
- Use the present perfect in the main clause when you have a time phrase with *since* or *for*. Use *since* with a specific date or time (*I have lived in this house since 1986*). Use *for* with a period of time (*Humans have used writing for thousands of years*).
- Don't use the present perfect with an exact time signpost. Use the past simple. For example: *Alexander Graham Bell invented the telephone in 1876.*
- Contractions of the verb *have* are common in conversation and informal writing (see Appendix B).

## The Next Step

- Another way to express a cause and effect relationship involving change is to use a special kind of coordinating conjunction: **as X rises, so does Y.** For example: *As interest rates rise, so does the cost of mortgages.*

## Exercise 4.1

*Underline the correct verb from the choices in parentheses.*

1. Native Americans (have lived / lived) on the American continent for as long as 10,000 years.

2. Hurricane Katrina (has hit / hit) New Orleans in 2005.

3. One hundred years ago, many babies died in their first year of life. Today, that (has changed / changed).

4. Scores on standardized school tests (have rised / have risen).

5. Many young people (have gone / have went) to live in big cities.

## EXERCISE 4.2

Read the passage about journalism.

---

Television has changed the way people understand war. During World War II, most ordinary people knew little about what was happening far away. They read reports about the war in the newspaper after the events happened. However, today, television and the Internet have brought wars into our living rooms. As a result, we have started to ask for more detailed news, and some news channels have sent their reporters into war zones. TV journalists say that we have become more knowledgeable about wars. However, some critics believe that we have lost our ability to feel shock because we have seen so much detail of recent wars and have therefore stopped caring about war.

---

Choose the best answer for the questions.

1. Which of these sentences best expresses the main idea of the paragraph?
   a. Most people don't watch news about wars.
   b. Our understanding of war has changed because of technology.
   c. Newspapers have always sent reporters into war zones.
   d. Nobody is shocked by wars anymore.

2. Which of these sentences is true according to the paragraph?

   a. In the past, we knew more about wars.

   b. In the future, we will know more about wars.

   c. We know as much about wars today as in the past.

   d. We know more about wars today than in the past.

3. Why does the author say, *some news channels have sent their reporters into war zones*?

   a. To show that TV is better than newspapers

   b. To give a reason for the change in wars

   c. To show the result of our increased interest in wars

   d. To give an example of good journalism

4. The paragraph gives two different opinions about the results of the increase of information about wars. Complete the chart by writing the correct opinions. You will not use two of the answer choices.

| TV journalists | 1. |
|---|---|
| Some critics of television | 1.<br><br>2. |

   a. We are not interested in wars.

   b. We don't know enough about wars.

   c. We know more about wars.

   d. Wars do not shock us.

   e. There are fewer wars today than in the past.

## Future Verb Forms

There is no real **future tense** in English. However, there are several different ways of talking about future events and situations. Although future verb forms are not common in academic writing, they do occur in speaking, and you might need them on the iBT to understand and make predictions about future effects of present causes.

> "If the university **cuts** out some programs, the quality of the education here **will suffer**. I mean, people **will stop** respecting us."
>
> —*The Michigan Guide to English for Academic Success and Better TOEFL® Test Scores*, p. 264

> *Because of the amount of carbon dioxide in the atmosphere, the climate **will** become warmer.*

The speaker is 100 percent certain about the effects of carbon dioxide on the climate and so uses *will*.

> *After I finish college, **I'm going to** apply to graduate school.*

The speaker has made a plan for the future. This is the meaning of *going to*.

> ***We're meeting** next week to discuss the sociology final.*

The **present progressive** is also used for future plans, but it is more common in speaking than in writing.

### The Next Step

> *If the cost of gasoline **increases**, people **will** want smaller cars.*

- This is called a **conditional sentence.** The second clause is certain to happen, but only on the condition that the *if* clause is true (see Unit 6).

### Watch Your Step!

- Don't use *will* for future plans that are already made.
- Don't use *will* in the *if* clause (not *\*if the cost of gasoline **will** increase*).
- In academic writing, it is common to use **simple present** tenses to show that something is true in the past, present, and future. For example: *When an acid is added to an alkaline, a salt forms.* Logically, the second clause happens in the future (it is a result of the *when* clause).

## Exercise 4.3

*Write the verb in parentheses in the correct form. There may be more than one correct answer. The first one has been done for you as an example.*

1. *(study)*    If teachers do not give grades, students <u>will not study</u> as hard.

2. *(grow)*    Industries are producing more goods. Therefore, the economy _____ over the next year.

3. *(smoke)*    My city is going to ban smoking in public places. Fewer teenagers _____ as a result.

4. *(decrease)*    When it rains on election day, the number of voters _____.

5. *(learn)*    If you _____ more vocabulary, you will read faster.

---

*Step Up Note: The independent writing and speaking tasks on the iBT sometimes ask you to make predictions about the future.*

---

## EXERCISE 4.4

Write sentences to answer the questions. A sample answer has been provided for the first question, but you should also answer it for yourself.

1. When you go to university, would you prefer to have a roommate or live alone? Why?

   <u>I'd like to have a roommate. If I live alone, I won't meet new people, and I will feel lonely. So, I'm going to apply to live in a dorm.</u>

   Your answer: _____

   _____

2. Which is more important for you: a job with a high salary (wage) or a job that you enjoy? Why?

   _____

   _____

3. What will be the biggest problem facing the world in the next ten years? Why?

_____

_____

4. In the future, everyone will speak the same language. Do you agree with this opinion? Why, or why not?

_____

_____

Now, practice saying a one-minute answer to each question.

## EXERCISE 4.5

Read the article from your university's student newspaper.

### University Will Charge for Gym

Starting next semester, there will be a small fee to use the gym. All students will pay this fee as part of their tuition.

Track 19. Listen to two students discussing the newspaper article.
Take notes as you listen. Answer the questions about the article and the conversation.

1. What is going to happen next semester?

   a. The university is increasing its tuition fees.

   b. The university is starting to charge a fee for the gym.

   c. The university is closing the gym.

   d. The man is going to leave the university.

2. Which of the following sentences is true?

   a. Both students agree with the new fee.

   b. Both students disagree with the new fee.

   c. The woman agrees with the new fee, but the man disagrees.

   d. The two students haven't read the newspaper article.

3. Why is the man upset?

    a. He wants to go to the gym.

    b. He doesn't have any money.

    c. He has a problem in his classes.

    d. He never goes to the gym.

4. Track 20. Listen again to part of the conversation. What will happen if the man does not pay the fee?

    a. He will leave the university.

    b. He will pay more tuition.

    c. Other students will pay more money.

    d. He won't go to the gym.

5. What is the man going to do later today?

    a. write a letter to the president

    b. write a letter to the newspaper

    c. go to the gym

    d. pay his tuition fees

**Step Up Note:** *In the speaking section of the iBT, you will see a question like Question 6. For practice, you can answer the question in writing, you can say your answer to a partner, or you can record your answer on cassette or computer.*

6. The man gives his opinion about the newspaper article. What is his opinion, and what is his reason?

_____

_____

_____

_____

## Vocabulary You Need

### Cause-and-Effect Signposts

Causes and effects (or reasons and results) often appear together. It is important to recognize their signposts to help you understand the organization of lectures and readings on the iBT. You also need to use this vocabulary when you are giving your reasons for an opinion on the speaking and writing tasks. Study the following cause-and-effect signposts.

| Cause Signposts | Effect Signposts |
|---|---|
| cause: *Unemployment causes many problems.*<br>because of: *Some diseases happen because of genes.*<br>be due to: *The student's difficulties were due to a lack of study skills.*<br>be responsible for: *Airplanes are responsible for some types of air pollution.* | result in: *The invention of the Internet resulted in many social changes.*<br>lead to: *In business, one poor decision can lead to failure.*<br>promote: *The government's plan will promote peace in the region.* |

You have already met these cause-and-effect signposts: *so, because, as a result, consequently, therefore* (see Units 2 and 3).

### Watch Your Step!

- *Because* is followed by a **clause** (a group of words containing at least a subject and a verb)
- *Because of* is followed a **noun phrase** (a noun and some other words but no verb).

## Exercise 4.6

*Read the sentences. Write C above the causes, and write E above the effects. The first two have been done for you as an example.*

         E                          C

1. <u>I like visiting Paris</u> because <u>the buildings are very interesting</u>.

2. Due to the <u>public holiday, classes are cancelled</u> on Monday.

3. <u>The election</u> resulted in <u>a clear win for the President</u>.

4. <u>The student is unhappy</u> because of her <u>grade</u>.

5. <u>Eating fruits and vegetables</u> promotes <u>good health</u>.

## EXERCISE 4.7

Track 21. Listen to the lecture about teenage depression.
Take notes as you listen. *Depression* is a feeling of extreme sadness that lasts for a long time. Use your notes to choose the best answer to the questions.

1. Which of the following is NOT a cause of depression, according to this lecture?
   a. relationships
   b. stress
   c. university admissions
   d. drugs

2. What is one possible cause of stress, according to the lecture?
   a. homework
   b. teachers
   c. parents
   d. teenagers

3. What does the professor say that depression can lead to?
   a. bad relationships
   b. suicide
   c. poor grades
   d. alcohol abuse

4. Which of the following sentences is true about stress?

   a. Stress always leads to depression in teenagers.

   b. Teenage depression is never a result of stress.

   c. Depression promotes increased stress in teenagers.

   d. Stress causes depression when teenagers can't manage it.

5. What does the professor conclude about depression?

   a. Teenagers need to have someone to talk to about depression.

   b. All teenagers get depressed.

   c. Teachers need to help students so that they don't get depressed.

   d. Parents are responsible for all teenage depression.

 **Exercise 4.8**

> *Step Up Note: Some questions on the speaking and writing sections of the iBT ask you to give reasons for an opinion. Explaining the cause or effect of an event is another way to develop your answers.*

*Continue each idea with a reason (a cause or an effect). Use the cause-and-effect signposts and the grammar from this unit to help you. The first one has been done for you as an example.*

1. Some companies are not advertising on television <u>because many people change channels during the ads.</u>

2. All children should play a sport _____

   _____

3. In the past, doctors did not know that germs caused disease _____

   _____

4. I think zoos are bad for animals _____

   _____

5. Economics should be a required subject for all high school students

   _____

## Cause or Correlation?

**Correlation** means that two things happen at the same time or in sequence. However, just because one thing happens after another doesn't mean that there is a cause-and-effect relationship. For example, imagine you are watching a soccer (football) game on television. You leave the room to get a drink, and then your team scores a goal. Your action (getting a drink) did not cause your team to score a goal! It is simply a coincidence.

In many sciences and social sciences, it is important to understand the difference between correlations and causes. Also, certain questions on the iBT listening and reading sections ask you to explain the relationships between ideas and recognize real causes.

---

**Correlation Signposts**

There is a *connection* between the moon and ocean tides.

The speaker doesn't say what kind of connection there is, just that a connection exists.

Suicidal thoughts often *accompany* depression.

This means that suicidal thoughts and depression often happen together. We don't know why.

There is a *link* between drinking tea and some chemicals that prevent cancer.

This sentence does not say that drinking tea will prevent cancer. It suggests that there is some connection, but not a strong cause and effect.

Rock and roll music *is associated with* the 1960s.

Here, we know that most people think about the 1960s when they hear rock and roll music.

The report *implies* that bullying is increasing in schools.

This is not a result of the report. It is a suggestion, and we can guess that the author of the report is not 100 percent certain that bullying is increasing.

---

Some other correlation signposts include: *at the same time, meanwhile, coincidentally.*

*Step Up Note: On the iBT reading and listening sections, you have to infer opinions or facts. This means you won't read or hear the information, but you can answer the question if you understand the passage well.*

iBT

## EXERCISE 4.9

Read the sentences from a reading passage on childhood obesity. Then, use the cause, effect, and correlation signposts to choose the sentence that best expresses the main idea.

1. There is a connection between childhood obesity and diabetes.
   a. Childhood obesity causes diabetes.
   b. Diabetes leads to childhood diabetes.
   c. Children who are obese often also have diabetes.
   d. Children who have diabetes are not usually obese.

2. Obesity sometimes leads to depression in children and teenagers.
   a. Depression causes obesity in some children and teenagers.
   b. Obesity causes depression in some children and teenagers.
   c. All obese children are depressed.
   d. There is no cause and effect relationship between obesity and depression.

3. A family history of smoking is associated with childhood obesity.
   a. The parents of some overweight children are smokers.
   b. Children are obese because their parents smoke.
   c. Some children smoke due to their obesity.
   d. Non-smoking parents don't usually have obese children.

4. Children today watch more television than ever before. At the same time, rates of childhood obesity have risen.
   a. Watching television results in obesity.
   b. If children do more exercise, they will not become obese.
   c. Children watch TV because they are obese.
   d. There is a connection between television viewing and childhood obesity.

5. Some studies imply that some drugs could treat obese children.
   a. There are good drugs to treat obese children.
   b. There are no drugs to treat obese children.
   c. Obesity promotes drug abuse.
   d. Studies have not proved the effectiveness of drugs for childhood obesity.

## Words to Learn

Some common and useful words from Unit 4 follow. Words marked with an asterisk (*) are from the Academic Word List.

| | | |
|---|---|---|
| admissions | critic | refuse |
| alone | depression, depressed* | region* |
| ban | event | reporter |
| bullying | fee* | technology* |
| channel* | invention | tuition |
| childhood | ordinary | wage |
| coincidence* | pollution | war |

 Speaking Clearly

### Reductions

When you listen to fluent North American speakers, you will often hear words that sound like *gonna, wanna, hafta* (meaning *going to, want to, have to*). These are not English words and you should never write them, especially on the iBT. They are, however, useful in the listening and speaking sections of the test because they are regular **reductions** in informal, spoken English. Reductions are less common in very formal, careful speech. Reductions occur because of three features of English:

1. We divide speech into **thought groups** (see Unit 3).

2. Each thought group usually has one major stress, so the other words are **unstressed** or less stressed (see Unit 3).

3. Unstressed syllables and words are often reduced by changing vowels to a **schwa** /ə/ sound (see page 27).

Look at this sentence. The thought groups are divided with a slash (/) and the major stress words are underlined:

*I'm going to <u>go</u> / to the <u>library</u>.*

*Going to* sounds like *gonna* because the two vowels are reduced to **schwas,** the –*g* often disappears at the end of –*ing,* and the /t/ sound is not produced after an /n/. Similar processes produce *wanna* (want to), *hafta* (have to), *otta* (ought to).

*Step Up Note: The paragraph in Exercise 4.10 could be the answer to an iBT integrated speaking task about preventing childhood obesity.*

## EXERCISE 4.10

1. Read the paragraph. Underline words that you expect to be reduced, and write the reduced form above it. The first one has been done for you as an example.

*gonna*
Teenagers aren't <u>going to</u> listen to doctors, so the government ought to use the Internet. If kids see a really good website about obesity, they're going to read it. An even better idea is to use an Internet video. Teenagers want to watch what their friends are watching, so the video's going to spread quickly. This shows that modern problems have to have modern solutions.

2. Track 22. Listen to the audio. Listen to the answer. Check your answer.

3. Practice speaking the paragraph with the audio.

## Linking

One feature of fluent speech is that we don't pause after every word. You have already seen that small words like *to* often join with other words (e.g., *gonna*). A similar process happens with other words, too, and we call this **linking.** There are three kinds of linking:

1. *consonant* → *vowel:* When a word ends with a consonant sound and the next word starts with a vowel sound, we link the consonant onto the next word. For example, *children eat* sounds like *childre-neat.*

2. *vowel* → *vowel:* When a word ends with a vowel sound and the next word starts with a vowel sound, we add a /w/ or /y/ sound to link the words. If the first vowel is *round* (your lips make an "O" shape when you say it), we add a /w/ (e.g., *you are* sounds like *you-ware).* If the first vowel is *tense* (your lips are flat and wide when you say it), we add a /y/ (e.g., *I am* sounds like *ah-yam).*

3. When two consonant sounds fall next to each other, the words run together. For example, *this sound* sounds like *thisound.*

## Watch Your Step!

- Remember we're interested in the sound, not the spelling. For example, *leave* ends in a /v/ sound even though it has a letter *e* at the end.
- Contractions count as a single word, so the last sound in *she's* is /z/.

### Exercise 4.11

*Practice saying these sentences. The linked sounds are underlined for you.*

1. He's asking hard questions.

2. I didn't hear the end of your sentence.

3. Go on to the next page.

4. The water heats up.

5. I'm making a solution.

6. She opens the box.

*Track 23. Listen to the sentences. Check your pronunciation.*

# UNIT 5

# Problems and Solutions

| Learning Targets | Importance on the iBT |
|---|---|
| Modals of certainty<br>Adverbs | • **iBT Reading and Listening:** modals and adverbs help answer questions about details, opinions, and the speaker's intentions<br>• **iBT Writing:** control the certainty of opinions for a more academic style<br>• **iBT Speaking:** make answers clearer and more interesting |
| Problem signposts<br>Solution signposts | • **iBT Speaking:** summarize a problem and suggest a solution<br>• **iBT Listening:** understand the problem and solution in service-encounter conversations<br>• **iBT Reading:** understand problems and solutions in an academic field<br>• **iBT Integrated Writing:** summarize and explain a problem (from a reading) and a solution (from a lecture) |
| Pronunciation of<br>*can / can't*<br>Intonation in lists | • **iBT Listening:** understand the words *can* and *can't*, which are difficult to distinguish but have opposite meanings<br>• **iBT Speaking:** list more than one example or several details to help the listener follow the organization of your answer |

## Getting Started

*Discuss these questions with a partner or friend, or freewrite your answers.*

1. Describe a problem you had recently. How did you solve it?

2. What is the biggest problem in the world today? How could you solve it?

3. Have you ever helped a friend solve a problem? What was the problem, and how did you help?

## Grammar You Can Use

### Modals of Certainty

"The power relationship between two parties **may** profoundly affect how a dispute is resolved. Imagine how differently a dispute between a peasant and a landowner **might** be resolved compared to a dispute between two wealthy landowners."

—*The Michigan Guide to English for Academic Success and Better TOEFL® Test Scores*, p. 237

A **modal** is a special kind of verb that shows the speaker or writer's attitude toward the main idea in the sentence. There are only a few modals in English, but they have many different functions. The **modals of certainty** *(can, could, may, might)* are common in academic reading and writing, so you will see and use them on those sections of the iBT. All of them except *may* are common in conversation, so you will hear and use these modals in the listening and speaking sections.

These modal verbs show whether you are very certain, quite certain, or not certain about something. Often, when you describe the solution to a problem, you cannot be 100 percent certain that you are right. Using a modal verb correctly shows that you are open-minded and fair.

Governments *can* reduce the cost of health care.

You *could* take the class again next semester.

The solution to the gasoline problem *may* be electric cars.

The professor *might* give you an extension on your paper.

*more certain*

*less certain*

 ### Watch Your Step!

- Modal verbs are always followed by the base form of the verb (the infinitive without *to*).
- Modal verbs do not agree with the subject (not *\*he cans)*, and they do not have tense (not *\*he has could*).
- The difference in certainty between *can* and *could* is quite small. However, *could* suggests something that is possible in the future. *Can* is more immediate.
- The most common modal verb in English is *can*. In academic writing, *may* is also common.
- *Will* is also a modal verb (see Unit 4). It means 100 percent certainty; for example, *You **will** feel better if you talk to a counselor.* In academic writing, it is unusual to be 100 percent confident, however.

*The Next Step*

- You can add tense to a sentence with a modal verb, but you change the main verb, not the modal. For example, *You could have asked me* (past time: in the past, *you had the chance to ask me*); *The problem might be getting worse* (progressive aspect: *at this moment, the problem is possibly getting worse*).

 **Exercise 5.1**

*Rewrite each of the sentences with a modal verb of certainty. The first one has been done for you as an example.*

1. The most serious difficulty for undergraduate students is writing.

   The most serious difficulty for undergraduate students may be writing.

2. A tax cut improves the quality of life.

   _____

3. Researchers will find a cure for cancer in the next 15 years.

   _____

4. According to historians, Arthur was a real British king.

   _____

5. The experiment proves Darwin's theory of evolution.

   _____

## EXERCISE 5.2

Track 24. Listen to the conversation between a student and his professor.
Take notes as you listen.

1. Place a check (✓) in the correct column in the table to reflect the information
   in the conversation. Whose opinions are these, the professor's or the author's?

| Opinion | Professor | Author |
|---|---|---|
| a. The Internet is the most important source of news. | | |
| b. The Internet might be the most important source of news. | | |
| c. TV networks will stop showing the news. | | |
| d. TV networks might continue to show the news. | | |
| e. A lot of people don't trust the Internet. | | |
| f. In five years, 65 million more Americans might have access to the Internet. | | |

2. Who do you agree with: the professor or the author of the article? Why? Take
   a short time to prepare your answer, and then speak for about a minute. If
   possible, talk to a friend or partner or record your answer.

*Step Up Note: Question 2 is a similar task to Question 5 on the iBT speaking sec-
tion, but the topic of the conversation on the test will be different.*

# Adverbs

**Adverbs** are words that describe verbs, adjectives, other adverbs, clauses, or whole sentences. An adverb cannot describe a noun—only an adjective does that. You have already met one group of adverbs: sentence connectors such as *however, therefore, first,* and *also* are adverbs because they add to the meaning of a sentence. Other adverbs describe *frequency* (e.g., *sometimes, often, rarely, always, never, usually*). Still other adverbs make words stronger (e.g., *really, very, too, so*).

> "The unemployment rate fell from 5.9 percent to 5.7 percent in July, which is good news. **Unfortunately,** this is not sustainable job growth because the new jobs were mostly the result of a one-time increase in government jobs."
>
> —*The Michigan Guide to English for Academic Success and Better TOEFL® Test Scores,* p. 239

The most important adverbs for this unit give opinions (e.g., *certainly, possibly, maybe, perhaps, definitely, frankly, unfortunately, only, likely, hopefully*). The iBT test might ask you about a writer or speaker's attitude about an idea.

---

*Unfortunately,* we cannot solve this problem *just* by spending money.

This tells you that money is not the only solution, and the speaker is unhappy about this.

*Maybe* you can take the course next semester.

The adverb changes the modal verb—the speaker is not very certain.

An apology is *definitely* a good solution.

The speaker is showing a very high level of certainty and is trying to persuade you.

---

## Watch Your Step!

- Don't confuse adjectives and adverbs. For example, *the student is **angry*** or *he talks **angrily.*** In the first sentence, *angry* is an adjective, and it describes the student. In the second sentence, *angrily* is an adverb because it describes how the student *talks.*
- In the iBT writing section, put a comma after an adverb at the start of a sentence.
- In speaking and writing, adverbs are usually found in the middle of sentences. However, linking adverbs generally go at the beginning (as in this sentence).

## The Next Step

- *Just* is one of the most common adverbs in conversation (although *just* is rare in academic writing). Sometimes, it makes the next word(s) stronger *(It's just awful!)*, sometimes it means "this is the only thing" *(Just fill out this form)*, and sometimes it makes a request or statement softer *(I just wanted to ask about the research paper)*. Understanding this word is especially helpful for pragmatics questions on the iBT listening test.

## EXERCISE 5.3

Read the passage about an environmental problem.

---

One of the biggest problems in many western countries is a lack of water. As cities grow, they need more and more water, and this is a particularly serious problem in dry places. To solve this problem, cities could perhaps take more water from rivers. However, this would certainly harm fish and other wildlife. Fortunately, there is another solution. Cities can take water from the sea and remove the salt. Most likely, this will be unpopular because the process is expensive. Hopefully, people will realize that the cheapest solution is not always the best one.

---

Choose the best answer to the questions.

1. Who is water a particularly serious problem for?
    a. western countries
    b. cities
    c. fish
    d. cities in dry places

2. What does the writer say about taking water from rivers?
    a. It is impossible.
    b. It is the best solution.
    c. It is a possibility.
    d. It is happening now.

3. What is the writer's opinion about the effects of taking more water from rivers?

   a. It might be harmful for fish.

   b. It could perhaps be harmful for fish.

   c. It will not be harmful for fish.

   d. It will definitely be harmful for fish.

**Step Up Note:** *In an iBT reading passage, a word or sentence may be highlighted as in the paragraph, and you will be asked a question just about that word or sentence on page 66.*

4. Which of the following best summarizes the meaning of the highlighted sentence?

   a. The author says there could be another solution.

   b. The author is happy that there is another solution.

   c. The author is not certain that there is another solution.

   d. The author thinks there is another solution.

5. What will be the public's response to using seawater, according to the passage?

   a. probably negative

   b. probably positive

   c. maybe negative

   d. maybe positive

6. Which of the following sentences best summarizes the author's opinion?

   a. There are no good solutions to this problem.

   b. Taking water from rivers is the best solution.

   c. Removing salt from seawater is the best solution.

   d. The cheapest solution is the best solution.

## EXERCISE 5.4

Track 25. Listen to the conversation between a student and a housing office assistant.

Take notes as you listen. Use your notes to choose the best answer to the questions.

1. Why does the student go to the housing office?
   a. to complain
   b. to ask for information
   c. to apologize
   d. to make a request

2. Why does the secretary say that she doesn't have any single rooms?
   a. She doesn't want to help the student.
   b. They are very busy this year.
   c. The student needs to fill out a form.
   d. It is impossible to change rooms.

3. Track 26. Listen again to part of the conversation. What is the student's attitude toward the secretary's suggestion?
   a. The student is excited.
   b. The student is angry.
   c. The student is certain.
   d. The student is unhappy.

4. Which of the following is certain?
   a. The student can fill out a form.
   b. The student will get a different room.
   c. The student will swap rooms with a friend.
   d. The student will not change rooms.

5. What is the secretary's attitude toward the student's request?
   a. The secretary thinks the student will probably get a single room.
   b. The secretary thinks the student's request is impossible.
   c. The secretary is not helpful to the student.
   d. The secretary thinks the student will probably not get a single room.

Vocabulary You Need

## Problem Signposts

Several types of question on the iBT require you to understand or explain a problem. There are many **synonyms** for *problem* (see Unit 4) that you need to recognize and use, as well as some related problem signposts. For example:

> The population is getting older, and this is a growing *problem*. The *difficulty* comes from the increasing cost of caring for seniors. Governments recognize this *issue* and are working to find solutions to the *challenge*, but it is a complex *matter* to resolve.

Note also these **collocations** (words that often go together):

| | |
|---|---|
| *have a problem* | *the only problem (with X) is . . .* |
| *present a problem* | *the main problem is . . .* |
| *be a problem* | *a larger problem is . . .* |
| *approach a problem* | *the problem with (X) is . . .* |
| *face a problem* | |
| *get into difficulty* | *present a difficulty* |
| *have difficulty (in) doing something* | |

Finally, these words have other important family members:

| Noun | Adjective | Verb |
|---|---|---|
| *difficulty* | *difficult* | |
| *problem* | *problematic* | |
| *challenge* | *challenging* | *challenge* |

### Exercise 5.5

*Read the paragraph about Internet telephones, and fill in the blanks. Use a different signpost for each blank.*

The main _____ with Internet telephones is their reliability.

Internet service providers are trying to solve this _____.

However, a bigger _____ is power cuts. It is

_____ to design an Internet telephone system that

will work when the power is cut. In addition, some people have

_____ in installing Internet telephones. Making Internet

telephones simpler is _____ but necessary.

*Step Up Note: Exercise 5.6 is similar to the first part of Question 4 on the iBT speaking section. On the test, you may also have to give your opinion about the problem.*

### EXERCISE 5.6

Track 27. Listen to the conversation between a student and her professor. Make notes about the student's problems. Summarize the student's problem in your own words. Take a short time to prepare your answer, and then speak for about 30 seconds. If possible, talk to a friend or partner or record your answer. You could use these phrases to help you:

*The woman is having a problem with . . .*

*One challenge is . . .*

*Another difficulty is . . .*

*. . . presents a major problem for her*

## Solution Signposts

In addition to understanding and discussing problems, you will need to understand and suggest solutions on the iBT test, especially in the speaking section. Some solution signposts that will help you are listed.

| Nouns | Verbs |
|---|---|
| *an answer* | *answer (a challenge)* |
| *a fix* | *fix (a problem)* |
| *a proposal* | *propose (an answer)* |
| *a resolution* | *resolve (an issue)* |
| *a response* | *respond to (a difficulty)* |
| *a settlement* | *settle (a problem)* |
| *a solution* | *solve (a problem* |
| *a suggestion* | *suggest (a solution)* |

### *Watch Your Step!*

- Notice that some nouns and verbs have the same form. Be sure to use them correctly.
- Some verbs, such as *respond*, need the preposition *to*.

### *The Next Step*

- You can make your solutions less certain with adjectives such as *possible, potential, theoretical* ( = in theory, may not be real), *proposed* ( = someone has suggested it).
- Another common structure in academic writing to introduce a solution is: *It is (not) possible to* (+ VERB) or *It should be possible to* (+ VERB). For example: *It should be possible to reduce the amount of electricity we use.*

**Exercise 5.7**

*Suggest a solution to each problem. Write one or two sentences using solution signposts. The first one has been solved for you as an example.*

1. Your friend is always late to class.

   <u>One solution is to get up earlier. She can also solve the problem if she sets her watch five minutes fast.</u>

2. You want to travel for a year before you go to college. Your parents don't approve of your plans.

   _____

   _____

3. You like to work in silence, but your roommate prefers to listen to the radio while he/she is working.

   _____

   _____

4. We are using too much gas because people drive everywhere, even short distances.

   _____

   _____

5. Your school wants to introduce a uniform, but the students refuse to wear it.

   _____

   _____

*Step Up Note: For the integrated speaking and writing questions of the iBT, you have to read a passage and listen to a lecture or conversation.*

## EXERCISE 5.8

Read the paragraph about a problem in psychology.

After World War I, many soldiers came home with no physical problems, but they clearly had emotional problems. They could not communicate with other people, or they were very nervous, or they could not sleep and eat normally. Doctors called this condition "shellshock."

Track 28. Listen to the lecture.
Take notes as you listen. Use the information in the reading and your notes to answer the questions.

1. In your own words, summarize the problem presented in the reading.

   _____

   _____

2. In your own words, summarize Sigmund Freud's solution, as explained in the lecture.

   _____

   _____

*Step Up Note: This part is similar to Question 4 on the iBT speaking section.*

What is shellshock, and how did Sigmund Freud try to solve it? Use information from the reading passage and the lecture in your answer. You have 60 seconds to speak. If possible, talk to a friend or partner or record your answer.

## EXERCISE 5.9

Track 29. Listen to the conversation between two students.
Take notes as you listen in on their problem and the possible solutions.

1. Describe the woman's problem in your own words.

   _____

   _____

2. What are the three possible solutions? Write notes below.

   ____ a. _____

   ____ b. _____

   ____ c. _____

3. Put a check next to the solution you prefer: a, b, or c. Why did you choose that solution?

   _____

   _____

4. Describe the woman's problem. Then say which of the solutions you prefer, and explain why. Speak for about 60 seconds. If possible, talk to a friend or partner, or record your answer.

> *Step Up Note: Question 4 in Exercise 5.9 is similar to Question 5 on the iBT speaking test. You will have 30 seconds to prepare and 60 seconds to respond on the test.*

## Words to Learn

Some common and useful words from Unit 5 follow. Words marked with an asterisk (*) are from the Academic Word List.

| | | |
|---|---|---|
| apologize | housing | reduce |
| attitude* | negative* | roommate |
| certain | positive* | source* |
| cure | prove | suggest |
| distance | provider | summary, summarize* |
| extension | psychology* | tax |
| fair | public | trust |

Speaking Clearly

## *Can* and *Can't*

You learned in this unit that *can* is a very common modal verb in speaking. Its negative, *can't*, is also important. However, the difference between *can* and *can't* is sometimes difficult to hear in American English because:

1. Words without the major stress in a thought group are unstressed (see Unit 3), and their vowels are often reduced to a schwa (/ə/) (see Unit 4). For example: *You can **ask** the professor.* The major stress is on *ask* so the vowel in *can* is reduced and the words sound like: /you cunASK/ .

2. Negative words such as *can't* are often stressed. However, /t/ is not pronounced after /n/. Therefore, *can't* sounds like *can*.

Therefore, if you hear a full /a/ vowel, you are probably hearing *can't*. If you hear a reduced vowel, you are probably hearing *can*. On the iBT speaking test, you can avoid the problem by saying *cannot* instead of *can't*. Be careful to reduce the vowel in *can*, however, or the listener might hear *can't*.

 ### Exercise 5.10

 Track 30. *Listen to the sentences. Circle* can *or* can't. *The first one has been done for you as an example.*

1. You *can / can't* see the effects of global warming.

2. There *can / can't* be an easy solution.

3. We *can / can't* try to use less energy.

4. Most people *can / can't* stop driving altogether.

5. Big companies *can / can't* make a difference.

**EXERCISE 5.11**

Track 31. Listen to the lecture about drinking and driving laws in the United States.

Take notes as you listen. The federal government is the national government of the United States. Each of the 50 states has its own government, too.

Place a check (✓) in the correct column in the chart to reflect the information in the lecture.

| | True | False |
|---|---|---|
| 1. You can't drink in the U.S. if you're 20 years old. | | |
| 2. The states can't choose the age limit for drinking alcohol. | | |
| 3. Michigan can choose 18 as the drinking age. | | |
| 4. If Michigan chooses 18 as the drinking age, the government will not give the state money to repair the roads. | | |
| 5. In theory, Michigan can pay for its own roads. | | |
| 6. Michigan has enough money to pay for its own roads. | | |

## Intonation in Lists

In some lectures on the iBT listening section, the professor might preview the topics in a list. For example: *I'm going to explain three problems: an economic problem, a social problem, and a political problem.* When you are summarizing a lecture or conversation on the integrated speaking tasks, you might also need to give a list like this.

Lists have a special intonation pattern. *Intonation* is the musical pattern of your voice: up and down. Each item in a list has *rising intonation* until the last item, which usually has *falling intonation.* You should also pause briefly after each item to help your listener follow the list. When you are writing a list with three or more items, you put a comma after each item, as you can see in the example in the preceding paragraph. If the list is at the start of the sentence (in subject position), you do not usually hear falling intonation in the last item.

### Exercise 5.12

*Track 32. Listen to the sentences. Draw arrows to mark rising intonation ( ⤴) and falling intonation (⤵) in the lists. The first one has been done for you as an example.*

1. Today's lecture is about Shakespeare: his life, his theater, and his plays.

2. There are three solutions to this problem: increase education, lower the requirements, or employ foreign workers.

3. Nuclear energy presents three major challenges: storing the waste product, securing the power plants, and protecting the population.

4. Salary, discipline, and testing are the three biggest problems for today's teachers.

5. A business can fail in many ways—it can choose the wrong location, it can set its prices badly, it can hire the wrong people, and it can promote itself poorly.

*Now, practice saying the sentences with the audio.*

**iBT**

### EXERCISE 5.13

Read the paragraph about language change.

Languages change through different processes. When languages are in contact, they change each other. Another type of change happens when the speakers of a language need a new word for something, such as a computer. The final type of change is internal change.

1. Complete the sentence to summarize the three processes of language change:

   Languages change for three reasons: _____,

   _____, and _____.

2. Read your sentence to a friend or partner or record your answer. Pay attention to the intonation of your list.

# UNIT 6

# Preferences and Opinions

| Learning Targets | Importance on the iBT |
|---|---|
| Modals of suggestion and necessity<br>Real conditionals | • **iBT Writing:** make complex sentences to give examples and explanations<br>• **iBT Reading and Listening:** understand professors' and students' opinions using modals and conditionals<br>• **iBT Writing and Independent Speaking:** give opinions |
| Opinion signposts (giving your opinion)<br>Hedging and softening signposts | • **iBT Writing and Speaking:** develop an argument fully on the opinion questions<br>• **iBT Listening and Reading:** understand when speakers soften their opinions and writers hedge their opinions<br>• **iBT Speaking and Writing:** hedge and soften opinions for a sophisticated academic style |
| Using intonation to show attitude<br>Discourse signposts (*um*, *ah*, and *wow*) | • **iBT Listening:** understand a speaker's attitude expressed by intonation; recognize a speaker's intentions with discourse signposts<br>• **iBT Speaking:** improve delivery score with correct intonation; increase fluency and cover errors with discourse signposts |

## Getting Started

*Discuss these questions with a partner or friend, or freewrite your answers.*

1. What is your favorite school subject? Why?

2. What is your favorite type of music? Why?

3. Which do you prefer: watching movies at the theater or watching them at home? Why?

Grammar You Can Use

## Modals of Suggestion and Necessity

You learned about modals of certainty in Unit 5. You can also use modal verbs to tell someone what you think they should do (**suggestion**) or what is necessary for them to do (**necessity**). You will see and use these modal verbs for opinions and preferences as well as advice. In addition to modal verbs *(must, should)*, there are other

"First, we **have to** read Chapters 6 and 7. For six, we're **supposed to** answer the questions at the end of the chapter. . . . And listen to this. . . . We **have to** go buy some packet in McBrain by 5:00 today."

—*The Michigan Guide to English for Academic Success and Better TOEFL® Test Scores*, p. 257

verbs that act like modals, called **semi-modals** *(have to, need to, be supposed to)*. Like modal verbs, they are followed by an infinitive, but unlike modals, you must use *to*, and the verb agrees with the subject *(He **has** to stop)*. Semi-modals can have tense, unlike modal verbs *(The army had to act fast)*.

*strong necessity*

Students *must* register before September 1.

Researchers *have to* ask permission from their subjects.

Governments *need to* provide clean water in poor countries.

You *should* come to the study session next week.

The university *could* change its rules.

*weak suggestion*

 *Watch Your Step!*

- *Must* is not common in conversation because it is very strong. *Have to* or *should* sound better. *Have to* is also possible in academic writing.
- *Should* and *must* are common in academic writing to express opinion without using *I* or *we*.
- Be careful with negative forms: *don't have to* means something is not necessary; *must not* means something is not allowed.

## *The Next Step*

- There are other semi-modals for this function, but they are rarely used. *Ought to* has a similar meaning to *should*. *Have got to* is similar to *have to*, but it is not used often in writing and is more common in spoken British English than American English.
- *Be supposed to* is useful in conversation. It means something is planned or expected *(You're supposed to see Dr. Smith in his office today)*.
- *Had ('d) better* occurs in conversation but not usually in writing. It means that you must do something, and if you don't do it, something bad will happen to you *(You'd better do your homework, or you'll fail the class!)*.

## Exercise 6.1

*Complete the sentences with a modal or semi-modal verb. Some of the verbs might be negative: it depends on your opinion! Make sure that semi-modal verbs agree with their subjects.*

1. You _____ make an appointment to see the doctor.

2. Children _____ listen to their parents.

3. Television producers _____ be more creative.

4. The government _____ ban smoking in public places.

5. People _____ carry cell phones (mobile phones).

## EXERCISE 6.2

Read the paragraph about nutrition. Nutrition means the food that you eat and the energy it creates for your body.

According to government nutritionists, we must balance the types of food we eat. Everyone has to eat grains (such as bread, pasta, or rice), but you should make half of the grains you eat whole grains such as whole-wheat bread. All people must have calcium every day. Calcium is an important source of nutrition found in milk. However, you don't have to drink milk; you can also get calcium from cheese or yogurt. People also need to exercise. Doctors say that we should all get at least 30 minutes of physical exercise every day.

Complete the chart with information from the reading. Copy the correct answer choices from the list. Two of the answer choices will not be used.

| Necessary | 1. |
| | 2. |
| | 3. |
| Recommended or optional | 1. |
| | 2. |

    a. balance the food we eat

    b. whole grains

    c. calcium

    d. sugars

    e. drink milk

    f. exercise

    g. use less oil

> **Step Up Note:** *In one of the integrated speaking questions on the iBT, you might read a university announcement and then hear students discussing it.*

### EXERCISE 6.3

Read the announcement from the university housing office:

---

All residents must follow the new noise rules. Undergraduate students need permission for parties of six or more people after 11:00 PM in a dorm room. Residents should not disturb their neighbors with loud music at any time.

---

Track 33. Listen to two students discussing the announcement.
Take notes as you listen. Use the information in the reading and your notes to choose the correct answer to the questions.

1. What is the students' attitude toward the new rules?
   a. They think the rules are clear and useful.
   b. They think the rules are easy to follow.
   c. They think there are too many rules.
   d. They think the rules are confusing and useless.

2. Which of the following situations is NOT allowed in the dorms?
   a. Seven undergraduate students in a dorm room at 9:00 PM.
   b. Six graduate students in a dorm room at midnight.
   c. Six undergraduate students playing music quietly at 11:30 PM.
   d. A resident talking on his cell phone at night.

3. Track 34. Listen again to part of the conversation. What does this sentence mean, according to the students: *Residents should not disturb their neighbors with loud music at any time?*
   a. It is a rule and everyone must follow it.
   b. Residents don't have to play loud music.
   c. It is a suggestion, not a rule.
   d. It's OK to play loud music during the day.

4. Why does the man say, "Cell phones must be turned off at night"?
   a. It is one of the new rules.
   b. He thinks it should be one of the new rules.
   c. He thinks students don't have to use cell phones.
   d. He thinks it is bad manners to make a call late at night.

# Real Conditionals

**Real conditional** sentences tell you what happens or happened in particular circumstances, or conditions. They are useful in the iBT speaking and writing questions when you want to give an example to support your opinion. You will also hear and read conditional sentences in the reading and listening sections used for the same purpose.

> "**When** I go to university, maybe I will feel lonely, but **if** I have a roommate, I can share lots of worries or problems so we can solve [them] together."
>
> —*The Michigan Guide to English for Academic Success and Better TOEFL® Test Scores*, p. 195

*If/when* you <u>live</u> in a small town, you <u>will meet</u> more people.

Students <u>learn</u> a new perspective *when/if* they <u>study</u> abroad.

*If/when* I <u>behaved</u> badly as a child, my parents <u>punished</u> me.

## *Watch Your Step!*

- The conditional clause (*if . . .* or *when . . .*) is a subordinate clause, and it follows the same punctuation rules as all subordinating conjunctions (see Unit 2).
- *When* and *if* have the same meaning in these sentences.
- Don't use *will* in the *if/when* subordinate clause. Apart from that, most combinations of present and past tenses are possible in real conditional sentences.

## *The Next Step*

- The **unreal conditional** is used for things that are not true but **could** be true under other conditions (*If I were the president, I would raise taxes*).
- The **unreal past conditional** is used for things that did not happen but **could have happened** under other conditions (*The tomatoes would have grown bigger if there had been more rain this summer*).

## EXERCISE 6.4

Read the paragraph about antibiotics. Antibiotics are a type of medication.

Some people have argued that doctors should not give patients antibiotics. For example, if you have the flu, you should not take antibiotics. If you take antibiotics for a minor illness, they may not work well if you have a serious illness later. However, in general, antibiotics are important medications. If patients really need antibiotics for serious illnesses, they should take them. Furthermore, patients should take all the antibiotics in the bottle. If patients do not finish the course of treatment, the illness will still be in the body, and patients will become even more ill later.

Choose the correct answer to the questions.

1. Which of these sentences best summarizes the author's opinion?
   a. Doctors should not give antibiotics to patients.
   b. The flu is not a serious illness.
   c. Doctors are giving antibiotics to too many patients.
   d. Antibiotics are useful treatments for serious illnesses.

2. When should you NOT take antibiotics?
   a. when the doctor gives you them
   b. when you are seriously ill
   c. when you become more ill
   d. when you have the flu

3. What happens if you take antibiotics for a minor illness?
   a. The antibiotics will not work.
   b. The antibiotics might not work the next time.
   c. Your doctor will be angry.
   d. You will catch a cold.

4. Which of the following pieces of advice does the author give?
   a. Finish all the antibiotics in a course of treatment.
   b. Go to the doctor when you have the flu.
   c. Stop taking antibiotics when you feel better.
   d. Do not take antibiotics when you are ill.

5. How can you get more ill, according to the passage?

   a.  if you do not take antibiotics

   b.  if you take too many antibiotics

   c.  if you do not listen to your doctor

   d.  if you do not finish the course of antibiotics

## Exercise 6.5

*Complete the real conditional sentences to support the opinion or preference in the first sentence. Punctuate your sentences correctly! The first one has been done for you as an example.*

1. University students should study a foreign language. <u>Most people write better in their first language</u> if they speak another language.

2. Instant messaging (IM) is a useful means of communication. If you need an immediate response from someone

   _____

   _____

3. I learned to drive this year, but before then I was dependent on my parents. I had to ask them when _____

   _____

4. People should not make illegal copies of music. If fewer people buy music legally _____

   _____

5. Living in a dorm is better than living at home as a university student. When you live in a dorm

   _____

   _____

## Vocabulary You Need

### Opinion Signposts (Giving Your Opinion)

Many of the iBT speaking and writing questions ask you for your opinion. You should use a range of vocabulary and expressions in your responses, so you cannot use *I think* and *in my opinion* all the time. In the listening and reading sections, you need to recognize when the speaker or author is giving an opinion (and not a fact). Here are some signposts that introduce an opinion:

> I **believe** that [college is not for everyone].
>
> I **have realized** that [fast food is harmful for our health].
>
> I **suggest** that [the man is right about the economy].
>
> I **suspect** that [water shortages are the biggest problem for the world].
>
> *Suspect means you think it's true, but you're not 100 percent sure.*
>
> **I agree/disagree with this idea.**
>
> **In my experience**, [language learning is more difficult for adults than children].
>
> **Personally**, I don't agree with [the rule].

| Opinion and Preference Signposts | |
| --- | --- |
| Positive Opinions (good) | Negative Opinions (bad) |
| *fortunately* | *unfortunately* |
| *hopefully* | *regrettably* |

### Watch Your Step!

- Native speakers don't generally use these expressions: *as I know; as we know; according to me; I know that.*

## EXERCISE 6.6

Track 35. Listen to the lecture about language learning.
Take notes as you listen.

1. Place a check (✓) in the correct column in the chart to reflect the information in the lecture. Do the sentences describe the "direct grammar" or "communicative language teaching" approaches?

|  | Direct Grammar | Communicative Language Teaching |
|---|---|---|
| a. Teachers must teach grammar. |  |  |
| b. Learners cannot reach a high level of language without grammar. |  |  |
| c. It is not necessary to teach grammar. |  |  |
| d. Teachers must teach communication skills. |  |  |

2. Which of the following sentences best expresses the professor's opinion about grammar teaching?
   a. We should always teach grammar directly.
   b. We should only teach communication skills.
   c. We should teach both grammar and communication skills.
   d. The experts on language learning are all wrong.

3. Why does the professor believe that teachers should teach some grammar?
   a. He agrees with the direct grammar experts.
   b. He disagrees with the communicative grammar experts.
   c. He has never been a language teacher.
   d. He has experience as a language teacher.

4. What is the professor's opinion about the two groups of experts?
   a. They will never agree, and he thinks this is bad.
   b. They will never agree, and he thinks this is good.
   c. They will eventually agree, and he thinks this is bad.
   d. They will eventually agree, and he thinks this is good.

*Step Up Note: These questions are similar to some iBT independent writing prompts.*

## EXERCISE 6.7

Give your opinion on the topics. Use opinion signposts. Write two or three sentences on each topic.

1. Governments should ban smoking in public places. Do you agree or disagree with this statement? Why?

   _____

   _____

   _____

2. Children learn more at home than at school. Do you agree or disagree with this statement? Why?

   _____

   _____

   _____

3. "Good fences make good neighbors." Do you agree with this saying? Why?

   _____

   _____

   _____

4. High schools' first responsibility is to teach students to pass tests. Do you agree with this opinion? Why?

   _____

   _____

   _____

5. It is not important to win a game. Taking part is more important. Do you agree with this idea? Why?

   _____

   _____

   _____

# Hedging and Softening Signposts

**Hedging** is a writing technique that helps you avoid statements that are too general, too strong, or too certain. Native speakers use a lot of hedging in academic writing when they give a personal opinion. You should use hedging on iBT independent writing questions that ask for your opinion.

**Softening** means making your speech more polite and less direct. You can use this on the iBT speaking section when are you giving your opinions.

Understanding hedging (on the iBT reading section) and softening (on the iBT listening sections) will help you recognize when a speaker is giving an opinion, stating facts, or expressing uncertainty.

| Hedging Signposts | Softening Signposts |
|---|---|
| *can, may, might* (see Unit 5) | *actually* |
| *frequently, often* | *maybe, perhaps* |
| *generally, in general, usually* | *kind of, sort of, a bit, quite* |
| *sometimes, occasionally* | *I guess* |
| *almost never, almost always* | *just* (see Unit 5) |
| *some / a few / many / most [people]* | |
| *slightly, somewhat, nearly* | |

## Watch Your Step!

- *Almost* is an adverb, which means you cannot use it in front of a noun.
  *\*Almost people* is not correct; we say *almost* **all** *people*.

## Exercise 6.8

*Read the pairs of sentences. Place a check (✓) next to the sentence that is more "academic" because it uses hedging or softening. Circle all the hedging and softening signposts. The first one has been done for you as an example.*

1. _____ a. Robots will certainly replace all teachers in the future.

   __✓__ b. Robots (may) replace (some) teachers in the future.

2. _____ a. Generally, pop music has slightly simpler melodies than classical music.

   _____ b. Today's pop music always has much simpler melodies than classical music.

3. _____ a. Nobody believes that any animal will ever learn to speak.

   _____ b. Most people believe that few animals can learn to speak.

4. _____ a. "The admissions secretary is so rude!"

   _____ b. "Actually, the admissions secretary is kind of rude."

5. _____ a. "Jim is failing the class because he's totally lazy."

   _____ b. "Jim is failing the class. I guess he's just sort of lazy."

**Step Up Note:** *The paragraph in Exercise 6.9 could be part of an essay you might write on the iBT independent task.*

## EXERCISE 6.9

Re-write the paragraph using at least one hedging signpost in every sentence.

### Does technology improve language learning?

Technology improves classroom learning. Computers help students improve all their language skills. Learners are more interested in the class when the teacher uses technology. We can do all class activities on computers. Furthermore, the Internet is useful for all homework assignments. In conclusion, we must replace all textbooks with technology.

## EXERCISE 6.10

Track 36. Listen to the conversation between a student and her professor. Take notes as you listen. Use your notes to choose the best answer to each question.

1. What is the main subject of the conversation?
   a. studying abroad
   b. getting a job
   c. graduation requirements
   d. the student's hometown

2. What does the professor mean when he says: "Well, I guess you could finish your requirements and graduate next semester."

   a. This is the best choice for the woman.

   b. This is a bad choice for the woman.

   c. The woman is allowed to make this choice.

   d. This is one choice for the woman but not the best choice.

3. Track 37. Listen again to part of the conversation. Why does the professor say this?

   a. He wants to know the woman's opinion.

   b. He thinks the woman's life experiences are limited.

   c. He is asking for the woman's opinion on this topic.

   d. He is criticizing the woman's life experiences.

4. Track 38. Listen again to another part of the conversation. What is the woman's attitude?

   a. She is nervous about discussing jobs with the professor.

   b. She is uncertain about the type of job she wants.

   c. She is excited about getting a job.

   d. She is comfortable discussing jobs with the professor.

5. What is the professor's opinion about her chances of getting a job?

   a. They will certainly be better if she studies abroad.

   b. They will be the same if she stays at her home university and finished her degree.

   c. They might be better if she studies abroad.

   d. She has a very good chance of getting a job.

## Words to Learn

Some useful words from Unit 6 follow. Words marked with an asterisk (*) are from the Academic Word List.

| | | |
|---|---|---|
| abroad | disturb | minor* |
| announcement | expert* | patient |
| appointment | illegal* | register* |
| avoid | illness | replace |
| creative* | limited | resident* |
| degree | manners | rude |

Speaking Clearly

## Using Intonation to Show Attitude

The iBT listening section includes questions about **pragmatics,** the practical use of language. They might ask you to identify the speaker's attitude—that is, the speaker's opinion or feelings. You can answer these questions using not only the words but also the intonation.

In the speaking test, good intonation can make your voice more interesting and improve your delivery score.

 ### Exercise 6.11

 *Track 39. Listen to the extracts. Then choose the attitude or feeling of the speaker. What emotion or attitude do you hear?*

|   |   |   |   |
|---|---|---|---|
| 1. | a. certain | b. unsure | c. unhappy |
| 2. | a. enthusiastic | b. angry | c. certain |
| 3. | a. confused | b. unhappy | c. sympathetic |
| 4. | a. frustrated | b. unsure | c. tired |
| 5. | a. selfish | b. angry | c. apologetic |

**Step Up Note:** *The questions in Exercise 6.12 are similar to the iBT independent speaking questions.*

 **EXERCISE 6.12**

Practice giving your opinion on the topics with as much emotion and feeling as possible. Use the grammar and vocabulary from this unit. Say your answers to a partner or friend or record your responses.

1. Watching television is a waste of time. Do you agree with this statement? Why?

2. Do you prefer to study in a library or in your room? Why?

3. Do we need a world language? Why?

## Discourse Signposts (*um, ah,* and *wow*)

Fluent, natural English conversation contains a lot of small words and sounds that have no meaning by themselves. However, they work as signposts for the speaker and listener to keep the conversation (**discourse**) going. Native English speakers do not like silence in conversation. It is better to fill the silence with something than to say nothing.

The iBT listening conversations use these signposts to sound natural. If you can use them correctly in the speaking section, you will sound more fluent and improve your delivery score.

| *Oh* | *Ah!* | *Wow!* | *Well* |
|---|---|---|---|
| something surprising, unexpected, new, or interesting | pleasant or unpleasant feeling | surprised and usually happy | tells the listener that you're thinking about the answer |
| *Oh, I think . . .*<br>*Oh, I see.*<br>*Oh, no.*<br>*Oh, yes.*<br>*Oh, right.* | *Ah, that's a great idea!*<br>*Ah, I hate that!* | *You got 100 percent on the test? Wow!* | *Well, I don't know.*<br>*Well, maybe.*<br>*Well, I think . . .* |

 *The Next Step*

- North American speakers also use *uh* and *um* to fill silences when they need time to think. However, don't use these **fillers** too much because they can be annoying to the listener. Don't use *ah* as a filler: the listener expects you to say something nice or unpleasant quickly.

> **Step Up Note:** *This conversation is similar to those you might hear on the iBT listening section.*

## EXERCISE 6.13

1. Read the conversation.

*Student (F):*    <u>Um</u>, hi. Um. I have a question about my tuition fees.

*Assistant (M):*   I'm sorry, we don't answer questions in person.

*F:*              _____ _____ I see. _____ _____ _____, how then can I ask my question?

*M:*              You need to send us an email, and we'll get back to you in, _____, 48 hours.

*F:*              _____ _____, that's a problem. _____, the bill is due tomorrow, and I think there's been a mistake.

*M:*              _____, alright. I'll take a look at it. _____ _____, that's not right. It should be $100, not $1,000.

*F:*              _____ _____. That's a big difference.

2. Track 40. Listen to the conversation between a student and an assistant in the registrar's office. Write the discourse markers in the blanks. The first one has been done for you as an example.

3. Read the conversation with a partner. Take turns to read both parts.

## Exercise 6.14

1. Read the conversation.

*Advisor:*  What subject would you like to major in?

*Student:*  _____

*Advisor:*  Why did you choose that?

*Student:*  _____

*Advisor:*  What would you like to do after college?

*Student:*  _____

*Advisor:*  Do you have any questions about your classes for next year?

*Student:*  _____

2. Track 41. Take the part of the student. Play the audio, and answer the questions during the pauses on the recording. Use discourse markers to help you speak without silences.

3. Practice the conversation with a friend or partner.

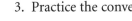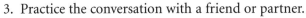

# UNIT 7

# Paraphrasing

| Learning Targets | Importance on the iBT |
|---|---|
| Adjective clauses<br>Subject-verb agreement | • **iBT Integrated Speaking and Writing:** define key terms from the reading and/or listening using adjective clauses<br>• **iBT Reading and Listening:** identify key words and definitions from adjective clauses<br>• **iBT Writing and Speaking:** control subject-verb agreement in all writing and speaking, including paraphrases |
| Definition signposts<br>Paraphrasing techniques | • **iBT Reading and Listening:** recognize definitions in lectures and passages<br>• **iBT Integrated Writing and Speaking:** write definitions; paraphrase ideas from reading passages and lectures |
| Pauses in non-restrictive adjective clauses<br>Endings with –s | • **iBT Listening:** understand the meaning of adjective clauses with and without pauses<br>• **iBT Speaking:** pause correctly in adjective clauses; pronounce plural endings and the third-person –s correctly to score high for accuracy |

## Getting Started

*Discuss these questions with a partner or friend, or freewrite your answers.*

1. What was the last book you read or movie you watched? What happened in the story?

2. What was the most important piece of advice you have had? Who gave you the advice? What did that person say to you?

3. What did you learn in class this week? Can you explain the idea?

Grammar You Can Use

## Adjective Clauses

**Adjective clauses** are a type of subordinating clause (see Unit 2). They are often used for definitions or to explain ideas. Like simple adjectives, adjective clauses give more information about nouns. There are two kinds of adjective clauses. **Identifying** (or, restrictive) adjective clauses give information that helps you *identify* the noun. **Non-identifying** (or, non-restrictive)

> "There are two major diseases **whose** sufferers benefit from this technology: diabetes and human growth hormone deficiency. People **who** suffer from diabetes used to rely solely on insulin **that** came from the pancreases of slaughtered pigs and cows."
>
> —*The Michigan Guide to English for Academic Success and Better TOEFL® Test Scores*, p. 157

adjective clauses give you extra information about the noun. Adjective clauses begin with **relative pronouns** such as *that, who,* and *which*. Like all pronouns (see Unit 3), relative pronouns refer back to the noun they describe (the **referent**).

| Identifying | Non-identifying |
|---|---|
| Hurricanes are tropical storms *that (which)* have winds over 75 mph. People *who (that)* study rocks are called geologists. | I'm taking linguistics, *which* is the study of language. The author, *who* is a Maori, describes the loss of her culture. |

 *Watch Your Step!*

- *That* can be used in any of these *identifying* clauses. However, it is not good style to use *that* with human nouns in academic writing such as the iBT® writing test.
- Notice the commas around non-identifying adjectives clauses.
- The verb in the adjective clause agrees with the referent (see page 102 in this unit).

### Exercise 7.1

*Combine the sentences using an adjective clause. The first one has been done for you as an example.*

1. There are two stages of sleep. The stages are called REM and non-REM sleep.

   <u>There are two stages of sleep, which are called REM and non-REM sleep.</u>

2. I was born in a small town. The town is famous for its cheese.

   _____

3. The tree was used to build canoes. It was the birch tree.

   _____

4. A National Park is an area of natural beauty. It is protected by the government.

   _____

5. The Ojibwe are a Native American tribe. They live in the Midwest and Canada.

   _____

---

***Step Up Note:** Adjective clauses are complex structures, so you should try to use them correctly in your answers on the writing section of the iBT.*

---

### EXERCISE 7.2

Rewrite the sentences using an adjective clause. Don't change or delete any of the ideas in the original sentences. The first one has been done for you as an example.

1. Anthropologists study ancient human societies.

   <u>An anthropologist is a person who studies ancient human societies.</u>

2. Snowshoes—a cross between a shoe and a ski—were an important means of transportation.

   _____

   _____

3. Some farmers began to rotate their crops, and these farmers were more successful.

_____

_____

4. Thomas Edison made nearly 100 designs for a light bulb. They didn't work.

_____

_____

5. S. E. Hinton is a very successful author, but she got poor grades for creative writing in high school.

_____

_____

6. The CPU is the brain of a computer. CPU stands for central processing unit.

_____

_____

## Exercise 7.3

*Write a definition for the terms using adjective clauses. You may need to research the answers in an encyclopedia or dictionary. The first one has been done for you as an example.*

1. psychiatrist: <u>A psychiatrist is a doctor who helps people with emotional and psychological problems.</u>

2. calcium: _____

_____

3. pixel: _____

_____

4. archeologist: _____

_____

5. peninsula: _____

_____

> **Step Up Note:** *One of the integrated skills tasks on the iBT listening section requires you to summarize a lecture in your own words.*

## EXERCISE 7.4

Track 42. Listen to the lecture.

Take notes as you listen. Use your notes to complete the summary of the lecture about Mackinac Island in Michigan. The first one has been done for you as an example.

Mackinac Island, which <u>is located between Lake Michigan and Lake Huron</u>, attracts a lot of tourists. Because there are no cars, tourists use other types of transportation, which _____.

A ferry, which _____,

takes tourists to the island. However, people who _____

_____ have to fly.

## EXERCISE 7.5

Read the paragraph about impressionism.

For many people, modern art begins with impressionism, which was a style of painting popular in France in the late 1800s. Impressionism, which comes from the French word meaning "feeling," tried to capture the emotion of the scene. Painters used a technique called **pointillism,** which involves making lots of small colored dots instead of large brushstrokes. The painter who best represents the movement is Claude Monet.  Monet lived in a quiet town that quickly become popular with other artists who wanted to learn from the great master.  His gardens, which are now a very popular tourist attraction, were the inspiration for many of his most famous paintings.

Choose the best answer to the questions.

1.  What is impressionism?
    a.  all modern art
    b.  a style of art
    c.  a period in French history
    d.  a famous artist

2. What was the aim of impressionist painting?

   a. to show real scenes

   b. to show people

   c. to show history

   d. to show feelings

3. What style of painting involves making many small strokes with the paint brush?

   a. pointillism

   b. impressionism

   c. Monet

   d. realism

4. Who was Claude Monet?

   a. a painting

   b. a painter

   c. a town

   d. a style of painting

**Step Up Note:** *You will see questions like Questions 5 and 6 on the reading section of the iBT.*

5. Which of the following sentences is the best summary of the highlighted sentence?

   a. Monet moved to a small town because there were many other artists there.

   b. Monet's town was already famous when he moved there with other painters.

   c. Monet lived in a quiet village, but soon other painters moved there to learn from him.

   d. All the famous impressionist painters lived together with Monet in a quiet town.

6. How are Monet's gardens used today?

   a. as a tourist attraction

   b. as an art school

   c. as inspiration for paintings

   d. as a museum

## Subject-Verb Agreement

"The biotechnology used in making insulin **is** more complicated than that used in making human growth hormone. The insulin molecule **is** made up of two polypeptide chains, which **join** to make the active form of insulin."

—*The Michigan Guide to English for Academic Success and Better TOEFL® Test Scores*, p. 17

In spoken and written English, the subject and its verb(s) must agree in person and number. For most verbs, this means that third-person singular verbs (used with *he, she, it,* or any singular noun) must have an *–s*. The verb *be* has more forms (*I **am**, he/she/it **is**, we/you/they **are***). Sometimes you need to look carefully to find the subject of a verb.

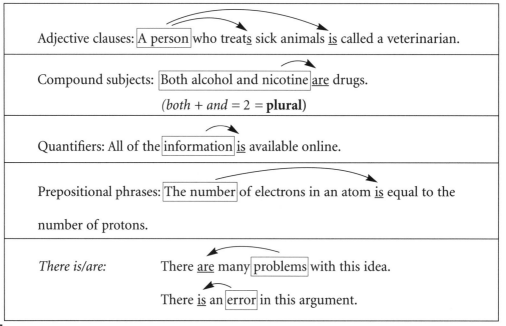

Adjective clauses: A person who treats sick animals is called a veterinarian.

Compound subjects: Both alcohol and nicotine are drugs.

(*both + and* = 2 = **plural**)

Quantifiers: All of the information is available online.

Prepositional phrases: The number of electrons in an atom is equal to the number of protons.

*There is/are:*     There are many problems with this idea.

There is an error in this argument.

### Watch Your Step!

- Modal verbs (see Units 5 and 6) don't agree with their subject. However, semi-modal verbs do (e.g., *he **has to** go*).
- Only *be* has a different third-person singular form in the simple past tense (*I **was**, you/they/we **were**, he/she/it/+ singular noun **was***).
- See Appendix B for contractions.

## Exercise 7.6

*Draw a box around the subject of the sentences, and fill the blanks with the correct form of the verb in parentheses. The first one has been done for you as an example.*

1. ⬚The population⬚ in less developed countries *is growing* faster than ever. (*grow,* **present progressive**)

2. There _____ three main sources of electricity: coal, gas, and nuclear power. (*be,* **simple present**)

3. The temperature of the Earth's oceans _____. (*rise,* **present progressive**)

4. Cars that have both gas and electric engines _____ called hybrid cars. (*be,* **simple present**)

5. Ostriches are a kind of bird that _____ fly. (*not, can,* **present**)

6. A student who _____ the class will need to take it again next semester. (*not, pass,* **simple present**)

---

iBT

## EXERCISE 7.7

Read this paragraph about sunburn.

---

When sunlight hits human skin, it can make it darker, and this is called a suntan. However, if a light-skinned person stays out in the sun for too long, he or she can get sunburn. Sunburn, which is a painful reaction to too much sunlight, can lead to serious medical conditions. Therefore, it is important to wear suntan lotion. Bottles of suntan lotion carry a number, which is the SPF, or sun-protection factor. This number shows how long it is safe to stay in the sun. For example, if skin will burn after ten minutes, a lotion with SPF 12 will protect the skin for 120 minutes, or two hours.

---

Now, complete the summary of the passage by filling the blanks with your own words. Make sure your verbs agree with your subjects.

1. Skin becomes darker when _____.

2. People can get sunburn if _____.

3. The SPF, or sun-protection factor, _____.

4. A suntan lotion with a high SPF

_____.

## Vocabulary You Need

### Definition Signposts

Readings and lectures on the iBT will often include technical words that you do not know. Some of these words are defined in the passage. Although you will not be tested on the meaning of these words, it is important to recognize definitions and understand key words.

When you answer the integrated speaking and writing questions, you might need to start with a definition of the topic. Definition signposts tell the reader or listener to expect a definition:

> X means / is defined as / is the same as / is known as Y
>
> X, which means / stands for Y, . . .
>
> X, or Y, is . . .
>
> Experts define X as Y / call X Y
>
> The definition / meaning of X is Y
>
> The technical / scientific / correct term / word / phrase / expression for X is Y

 **Exercise 7.8**

*Read the sentences, and circle the definition signposts. Underline the definitions. The first one has been done for you as an example.*

1. Sociolinguistics, (which is) the study of language in society, is a relatively new academic field.

2. Filmmakers call the scenes that they film in one day the *dailies*.

3. Digital camera lenses are measured in how many thousands of tiny dots they record, or megapixels.

4. ABS, which stands for anti-lock braking system, is standard in most new cars.

5. The meaning of hubris for the ancient Greeks was extreme pride and confidence in human ability.

*Step Up Note: The strategy in Exercise 7.9 is a good one for starting a summary in one of the integrated skills tasks on the iBT.*

**iBT**

## EXERCISE 7.9

Re-write the definitions in Exercise 7.8 using different definition signposts. The first one has been done for you as an example.

1. Sociolinguistics, or the study of language in society, is a relatively new academic field.

2. _____

   _____

3. _____

   _____

4. _____

   _____

5. _____

   _____

## EXERCISE 7.10

Read the paragraph about price controls.

A free market is defined as a market that allows the free movement of prices up or down. In most free markets, prices change according to the supply and demand of a product. However, sometimes a price might become too high for many consumers. Therefore, some governments use price controls. The definition of price controls is the range of prices that a product is allowed to cost.

Track 43. Listen to the professor talk about price controls.
Take notes as you listen. Use the information in the reading and your notes to complete the tasks.

1. Match the terms on the left with the definitions on the right. The first one has been done for you as an example.

   a. free market            the government fixes the range of a product's price

   b. price controls         a lack of something

   c. profit margin          allows the free movement of prices up or down

   d. shortage               the amount of money a company makes on a sale

2. The reading defines price controls, and the lecture discusses a problem with price controls. Put the events in order from 1 to 6. The first one has been done for you as an example.

   a. _____ Prices become even higher.

   b. _____ The government sets a price control.

   c. __1__ There is a shortage of the product.

   d. _____ The price of a product becomes too expensive for customers.

   e. _____ Companies stop making the product.

   f. _____ Companies can't make money on their product.

*Step Up Note:  Question 3 here is similar to Question 4 on the iBT speaking section.*

3. Use your answers to Questions 1 and 2 to explain what price controls are and why they are not successful. Say your answer to a partner or friend or record your answer. Use definition signposts to explain each stage of the process.

## Paraphrasing Techniques

The iBT integrated speaking and writing questions ask you to summarize or paraphrase a reading and/or a lecture. This means you have to explain the ideas in your own words. If you copy the words of the reading or lecture exactly, you will get a very low score. Here is one method you can use to paraphrase ideas:

1. Read the passage carefully several times. You can only listen to a lecture once on the test, but for practice, listen more than once. Take notes on the reading or lecture. Don't try to write full sentences—just write key words.

2. Think of synonyms (similar words—see Unit 3) for some of the key words.

3. Turn over the reading or turn off the audio. Use your notes to write a summary without looking at or listening to the original.

4. Compare your summary to the original reading or lecture. If there are many similar words or phrases, replace them with synonyms or different expressions.

### Watch Your Step!

- It is not enough to change one or two words in a sentence. You need to make the whole sentence look different.
- It is okay to keep some key words from the original, especially technical terms that are defined in the reading or lecture. However, you should write the definition in your own words.

## EXERCISE 7.11

Read the paragraph about saving energy.

If you own a house, you could save a lot of money—and help the environment—by reducing your energy use. The simplest way to reduce your energy use is to replace your old light bulbs with compact fluorescent light bulbs, which are more efficient, use less electricity, and last longer. A larger change that will save you money and energy is to replace your windows with a special type of glass that keeps heat in your house. The final change we suggest is the biggest: install solar panels (devices that convert the sun's energy into electricity) to power your home. If you save energy, you will save money and save the Earth!

1. Read the paragraph again, and complete the notes. Don't write full sentences.

    Reduce energy use—3 ways:

    a. Old light bulbs → _____ (more efficient,

    _____, _____)

    b. _____ (keeps heat in house)

    c. Install _____

    (Definition: _____)

    Save energy = _____ + _____

2. Find good synonyms for the following words and phrases in the context of this reading passage. Your synonyms can be simple, common words. The first two have been done for you as examples.

**Words**

reduce = <u>lower</u>

replace = _____

use (electricity) = _____

way = _____

install = _____

convert = _____

**Phrases**

save money = <u>spend less</u>

power your home = _____

save the Earth = _____

3. Use your notes and the synonyms to complete the summary of the reading passage. Use your own words: don't copy from the original text!

There are three good methods for lowering your electricity bill. First,

_____ because

_____.

Second, _____ with a glass that does

not let heat escape. Third, _____ solar panels,

which _____.

If you use less energy, _____

_____.

4. Finally, check your paraphrase against the reading passage to make sure it is different.

### Exercise 7.12

*Repeat the process in Exercise 7.11 to summarize this paragraph about voting in your own words.*

---

It is very important for university students to vote in elections. Voting allows everyone to express their opinions on the most important issues of the day. The easiest way to vote is to register in the town where your university is located. Then, you go to the voting station on election day. If you don't register in time, you have to vote in another way. The second way to vote is by mail. You need to request a voting form and return it in advance, however. The third way to vote is by proxy, which means asking someone to vote for you. Before you vote by proxy, you need to sign a document that gives the other person permission to vote for you. The way you vote is not important, but it is important that you vote!

---

_____

_____

_____

_____

_____

_____

## Words to Learn

Some useful words from Unit 7 follow. Words marked with an asterisk (*) are from the Academic Word List.

| | | |
|---|---|---|
| central | expect | relatively |
| coal | farmer | scene |
| confidence | island | standard |
| efficient | lake | sunburn |
| election | market | temperature |
| environment* | painting | transportation* |
| escape | protect | tribe |

Speaking Clearly

## Pauses in Adjective Clauses

In writing, you show the difference between identifying and non-identifying adjective clauses with commas. When you are speaking, you use pauses to show this difference. In an identifying adjective clause (no commas), you don't pause between the noun and the adjective clause. In a non-identifying clause, you pause slightly after both commas, and the pitch of your voice drops a little for the adjective clause. Remember that the pitch of your voice goes *up* before a comma and *down* at the end of sentence.

DVD, / which means digital video disk, / has replaced the video cassette.

 **Exercise 7.13**

*Mark the pauses and intonation in the adjective clauses in the sentences using arrows and slashes. Some clauses do not have pauses or special intonation. The first one has been done for you as an example.*

1. The American Revolution, / which happened in 1776, /
   marks the birth of the United States.

2. Britain, which had controlled America, went to war as a result.

3. An army leader, who was called George Washington, became the first president.

4. There were still people who wanted to be part of Britain.

5. The Americans won the war, which is known today as the War of Independence.

 *Practice saying the sentences.*

*Track 44. Listen to the audio. Listen to the correct pauses and intonation. Check your answers.*

**Step Up Note:** *The prompts in Exercise 7.14 are similar to the iBT independent speaking tasks.*

### EXERCISE 7.14

Tell a partner or friend your answers to the following questions, or record them on a cassette or computer. Try to use adjective clauses with the correct pauses and intonation. Plan your answer by writing some adjective clauses in the space provided. Try not to write complete sentences. Some sample clauses have been written for you as examples, but you should also answer for yourself.

1. If you could have any job, what would it be? Describe the job and say why you want to do it.

   a job that I have always wanted

   a veterinarian, who is a doctor for animals

   works with animals who are sick

   my uncle, who is a vet, encouraged me

   Your notes:

   _____

   _____

   _____

   _____

2. Describe a sport, activity, or hobby that you are interested in. Say how you do the activity and why you like it.

   _____

   _____

   _____

   _____

3. Describe a traditional holiday in your country. What happens?

   _____

   _____

   _____

   _____

## −s Endings

The −s ending occurs with plural nouns (e.g., *books*) and third-person singular verbs (e.g., *reads*). There are three ways to pronounce the −s ending. The pronunciation changes according to the last sound before the −s. The three pronunciations are /s/, /z/, and / ɪz /.

### Exercise 7.15

*Track 45. Listen to the words. Write them in the correct column of the chart. The first three have been done for you as examples.*

| eats | reads | watches | chooses | books | goes | has |
| --- | --- | --- | --- | --- | --- | --- |
| wakes | rides | studies | advises | says | tells | writes |

| /s/ | /z/ | /ɪz/ |
| --- | --- | --- |
| eats | reads | watches |
|  |  |  |

*Complete the rules for pronouncing the −s ending by checking the correct boxes.*

1. Last sound before −s ending is voiced
   (*d, b, g, l, r, m, n,* or any vowel sound)     ☐ /s/   ☐ /z/   ☐ /ɪz/

2. Last sound before −s ending is unvoiced (*t, p, k*)   ☐ /s/   ☐ /z/   ☐ /ɪz/

3. Last sound before −s ending is /s/, /z/, /ch/, /j/   ☐ /s/   ☐ /z/   ☐ /ɪz/

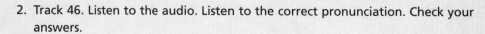

Step Up Note: *The paragraph in Exercise 7.16 could be the answer to an integrated speaking task on the iBT. The student has to explain the difference between the opinions in a lecture and a reading.*

## EXERCISE 7.16

1. Read the paragraph, and write the correct pronunciation (/s/, /z/, /ɪz/) above all the underlined plural nouns and singular verbs.

---

The professor explain**s** that he often catch**es** cold**s** on airplane**s**. He say**s** that germ**s** in the air spread disease**s**. However, the author disagree**s** with this opinion. He argue**s** that no one get**s** sick from air travel. The research support**s** his claim**s**.

---

2. Track 46. Listen to the audio. Listen to the correct pronunciation. Check your answers.

3. Practice reading the paragraph aloud.

# UNIT 8

# Sources of Information

| Learning Targets | Importance on the iBT |
|---|---|
| Reported Speech<br>Possessives | • **iBT Integrated Speaking and Writing:** report professors' and writers' opinion using reported speech and possessives |
| Source signposts<br>Opinion signposts<br>(describing other<br>people's opinions) | • **iBT (all sections):** recognize the source of information and opinions<br>• **iBT Integrated Speaking and Writing:** compare two different sources and discuss the opinions |
| Pronouncing the /th/<br>sound<br>Asking questions | • **iBT Speaking:** pronounce the difficult /th/ sound correctly for a better delivery score<br>• **iBT Listening:** understand speakers who use questions to disagree with another source<br>• **iBT Integrated Speaking and Writing:** use questions to move between ideas |

## Getting Started

*Discuss these questions with a partner or friend, or freewrite your answers.*

1. Describe the beginning of a recent class or meeting. Who spoke and what did they say?

2. Do you ever disagree with your brother, sister, parents, or other family member? What do you disagree about?

3. What questions do you have about preparing for TOEFL® iBT?

# Grammar You Can Use

## Reported Speech

"The author **states that** liberals believe in capitalist production, but **that** they also **believe that** the government must always punish those who break the rules or act unfairly."

—*The Michigan Guide to English for Academic Success and Better TOEFL® Test Scores*, p. 152

When you describe what someone said in different words or without using direct speech, you need to use **reported speech.** This is useful for paraphrasing (see Unit 7), describing conversations, and comparing different opinions on the iBT writing and speaking sections. When you read or hear reported speech on the test, make sure you understand *who* first had these ideas.

| Direct Speech | Reported Speech |
|---|---|
| I am going to collect your assignments. | The professor <u>said that</u> he **was going** to collect our assignments. |
| Tuition fees increased last year. | The student <u>said that</u> tuition fees **had increased** last year. |
| Drinking tea is good for the heart. | The author <u>wrote that</u> drinking tea **is** good for the heart. |

### Watch Your Step!

- When the reported speech is about a specific event or time, it is common to change the tense **back** one step. Therefore, simple present becomes simple past, simple past becomes past perfect, *will* becomes *would*, etc.
- However, when the reported speech is about a general truth, we often keep the original tense (usually the simple present).
- The word *that* can be deleted without changing the meaning of the sentence.
- Remember to change the pronouns as well (e.g., *you* to *us*).

### The Next Step

- Some verbs of reporting require an indirect object; for example, *The professor told **us** that . . .* (not *\*The professor told that . . .*).

## Exercise 8.1

*Change the sentences to reported speech. The sentences are labeled* lecture, conversation, *or* reading. *The first one has been done for you as an example.*

1. [conversation] Professor Smith is sick.

   <u>The teaching assistant said that Professor Smith was sick.</u>

2. [reading] The university is changing its attendance policy.

   _____

3. [lecture] We are going to talk about modern art.

   _____

4. [reading] Acidity is measured on the pH scale.

   _____

5. [lecture] Washington was the first U.S. president.

   _____

6. [conversation] I'll meet you at the library.

   _____

**Step Up Note:** *On the iBT integrated skills tasks, the reading and lecture may disagree with each other and present opposite points of view.*

## EXERCISE 8.2

Read the passage about single-sex education. Single-sex education means that boys go to school only with boys, and girls go to schools where there are only girls.

Research has shown that boys and girls get higher test scores when they go to single-sex schools. The difference is greatest for girls, who scored much better in math and science in a 1996 study than girls who went to mixed-gender schools.

Track 47. Listen to the lecture.

Take notes as you listen. Complete the chart by writing the answer choices in the correct row and in reported speech. The first one has been done for you as an example.

| Reading | 1. The author wrote that single-sex schools have higher test scores. |
| | 2. |
| Lecture | 1. |
| | 2. |

a. Single-sex schools have higher test scores.

b. Girls are less nervous in mixed schools.

c. In a 1996 study, girls got better scores in math and science.

d. Boys feel more motivated in mixed schools.

## Possessives

There are three ways to show possession in English. You can sometimes use **possessive pronouns** *(my, your, his, her, its, our, their).* When you are talking about a person or a time, you can use an **apostrophe** *('s) (Professor Head's class; tomorrow's lecture).* In most other cases, an *of* phrase is best *(the end of the book).*

Understanding possessives will help you find the sources in the listening and reading sections of the iBT, and you will need to use possessives in many types of speaking and writing.

"At 'We the **People's** Forum', which was the follow-up **of** the declaration for a culture **of** peace, six factors were discussed under the rubric **of** peace. Notice these formulations all expand the definition **of** violence from direct forms **of** violence to another type **of** violence called structural violence."

—*The Michigan Guide to English for Academic Success and Better TOEFL® Test Scores,* p. 260

 *Watch Your Step!*

- When you use an apostrophe after a plural noun, do not add another *s* (e.g., *the teachers' room*).
- When you use an apostrophe after a name ending in *s*, it is common to add another *s* (e.g., *Charles's opinion*).
- Be careful with subject-verb agreement when using long *of* phrases—see Unit 7 (e.g., **The author** *of many books about plants* **is** *visiting the university today.*).
- English speakers prefer to keep the first part of possessive noun phrases short by using *of*: for example, *We received the applications of many qualified candidates* is better than *We received many qualified candidates' applications.*

### Exercise 8.3

*In each sentence, circle the person or thing that has the possession, and underline the person or thing that is possessed. The first one has been done for you as an example.*

1. <u>The title</u> of (the book) is *The Language Instinct*.

2. Jane's roommate is a history major.

3. Tonight's homework is on page 36.

4. The professor gives her opinion about animal testing.

5. In the words of the current university president, we need a "global focus."

### Exercise 8.4

*Complete the sentences with a possessive phrase using the words in parentheses. Use pronouns to avoid repeating a noun. The first one has been done for you as an example.*

1. (students / textbooks) Students should bring <u>their textbooks</u> to the next class.

2. (yesterday / newspaper). Did you read the story about nuclear power in _____?

3. (data / analysis) An _____ shows problems with the theory.

4. (the professor / office hours) Why don't you talk to the professor during _____?

5. (Shakespeare / theater) _____ was called The Globe.

Vocabulary You Need

## Source Signposts

Source signposts tell you where the writer or speaker found the information or opinions. You need to recognize them so that you can answer questions about sources on the iBT reading and listening sections. You should also use a variety of source signposts in your answers to the iBT integrated speaking and writing tasks.

| Source Signposts (Reading) | | Source Signposts (Listening) | | |
|---|---|---|---|---|
| *author* *writer* | | *speaker* *professor* *lecturer* | | Words to describe the creator of the material |
| *text* *reading* *passage* | *book* *notice* *article* | *lecture* *conversation* *speech* | *discussion* *announcement* | Words to describe the event |
| *expert(s)* *researcher(s)* *scientist(s)* | | | | Words for people who do research |
| *study* *research* *data* (plural) | *report* *review* | | | Words for the product of research |

 **Watch Your Step!**

- Verbs like *say, tell, explain,* and *suggest* can have human or non-human subjects. For example, *the study suggests that, the reading says, the lecture explains.*

 **Exercise 8.5**

*Complete the sentences with source signposts. Use a different signpost for each blank. The first one has been done for you as an example.*

1. The <u>professor</u> explained that Chicago was called the Windy City because of its politicians.

2. The _____ says the Great Chicago Fire destroyed almost all the buildings in the city.

3. According to the _____ , only the Water Tower remained standing.

4. _____ have found that the fire started in a barn.

5. In *The Devil and the White City*, the _____ wrote about Chicago's successful World's Fair.

## EXERCISE 8.6

Track 48. Listen to the lecture about microwave ovens.
Take notes as you listen. Place a check (✓) in the correct column in the chart to reflect the information in the lecture.

Whose opinions are these?

| Opinion | Lecturer | Textbook | Experts/Research |
|---|---|---|---|
| 1. It is not safe to put any plastic containers in the microwave. | | | |
| 2. The textbook gives bad advice. | | | |
| 3. Some plastics can melt in the microwave. | | | |
| 4. All plastics release harmful chemicals. | | | |
| 5. The quantities of these chemicals are not dangerous. | | | |
| 6. We can sometimes use microwave-safe containers. | | | |

*Step Up Note: Exercise 8.7 is similar to the integrated skills tasks on the iBT speaking section. In the real test, you either read a notice and hear a conversation or just hear a conversation.*

## EXERCISE 8.7

Read the notice from your university.

# Attention All Students!

The Department of Languages is offering a new course in American Sign Language (ASL) next semester. You can register online for this class. "ASL is a fascinating language," says the instructor, Dr. James. According to the University Career Services, "ASL is an important skill in many jobs."

Imagine you are telling a friend about the notice. Tell your friend about the ASL class, and explain the reasons the notice gives for taking the class. Say your answer to, friend or partner or record it on a cassette or computer. Use source signposts in your response.

# Opinion Signposts (Describing Other People's Opinions)

In iBT readings and lectures, you might notice that different opinions are contrasted. The words used to introduce the reported speech and opinions sometimes tell you the speaker or writer's own opinion.

You can use these signposts in the integrated writing and speaking tasks to compare a listening and reading (see also Unit 6).

The professor **argues** that the problem is getting worse. *(= she gives reasons)*

The author **claims** that newspapers are dying. *(= he says this but you don't agree)*

Most students **assume** that they will get a job after graduation. *(= they believe this, but they don't have any reasons or support for this opinion)*

The research **proves** that bilingual children do well at school. *(= this is a fact; you are convinced that there is no doubt)*

The lecturer **points out** that the crime rate has actually decreased. *(= introduces a fact which supports her opinion or contradicts another opinion)*

**According to the lecture,** the climate is changing. *(= this opinion comes only from the lecture)*

**The author's opinion is** that Lincoln was the greatest U.S. president. *(= this is her opinion; there may be other opinions)*

## Exercise 8.8

*Complete the sentences with signposts from the box. Do not use the same word more than once. Choose the correct agreement for the verbs (see Unit 7).*

| argue(s)   claim(s)   assume(s)   prove(s)          according   opinion |
|---|

1. Some people _____ that all fats are bad for you. However, experts say that some types of fat are important for good health.

2. The woman _____ that it is better to go straight to college after high school, but I think it can be valuable to take a year off before college.

3. _____ to the writer, rates of childhood asthma are increasing.

4. The research _____ that there is a connection between poverty and educational achievement.

5. The professor's _____ is that competitive sports can be damaging to high school students.

**EXERCISE 8.9**

Read the paragraph about personality development.

## The Nature Argument

Personality, like all aspects of human life, is controlled by DNA. DNA is the total of all the genes in the human body, and it decides hair color, eye color, sex, and height. However, DNA also determines personality characteristics such as shyness, abilities such as playing a musical instrument, and even behaviors such as crime. A recent study found a gene that predicts future criminal behavior in some children.

1. Complete the four sentences to paraphrase the main ideas of the reading. Try to use your own words.

   a. The writer explains that DNA _____

   _____

   b. According to the reading, genes decide if a person is _____

   _____

   c. The author claims that musical ability _____

   _____

   d. Research proves that _____

   _____

Track 49. Listen to the lecture.
Take notes as you listen.

2. Complete the sentences, which paraphrase the information in the lecture. Use opinion signposts.

a. _____ DNA decides appearance.

b. _____ children with the "outgo-ing" gene may be shy if their parents do not care for them well.

c. _____ a musical gene is useless without practice.

d. _____ the crime gene does not always determine if a person will commit crimes as an adult.

e. _____ personality development depends on both nature and nurture.

3. The professor who gives the lecture disagrees with the ideas in the reading passage. Look at your answers from Questions 1 and 2 in this exercise. Find the ideas that are different in the reading and the lecture and connect those answers in the chart. The first one has been done for you as an example.

| Question 1 | Question 2 |
|:---:|:---:|
| a. | a. |
| b. | b. |
| c. | c. |
| d. | d. |
|  | e. |

*Step Up Note: Question 4 here is similar to the integrated writing task on the iBT. You might have to show how the lecture supports the reading, challenges the reading, or answers a problem presented in the reading.*

4. Write a paragraph explaining how the lecture agrees and disagrees with the reading passage. Use your answers to Questions 1, 2, and 3 to help you, as well as the vocabulary in this section. Do not copy directly from the reading or lecture; try to use your own words.

_____

_____

_____

_____

_____

## Words To Learn

Some useful words from Unit 8 follow. Words marked with an asterisk (*) are from the Academic Word List.

| | | |
|---|---|---|
| analysis* | crime | president |
| appearance | criminal | quantity |
| application | department | rate |
| attendance | microwave | safety |
| bilingual | personality | specific* |
| characteristic | politician | tendency |
| container | | |

 Speaking Clearly

### Pronouncing the *th* sound

The *th* sound is difficult for some learners because it does not exist in many other languages. There are in fact two different sounds for the letters *th:* a voiced sound, which we write as /ð/, and an unvoiced sound, which we write as /θ/. To tell the difference, put your hand on your throat and say *this* slowly. You should feel your throat vibrate. Now, say *thin.* You won't feel the vibrations. The sound in *this* is /ð/, and the sound in *thin* is /θ/. To make both sounds, make sure your tongue is slightly between your teeth.

## Exercise 8.10

*Track 50. Listen to the words. Do you hear /ð/ as in this, or /θ/ as in thin? Check the correct box.*

|  | /ð/ | /θ/ |
|---|---|---|
| 1. that | ☐ | ☐ |
| 2. think | ☐ | ☐ |
| 3. their | ☐ | ☐ |
| 4. the | ☐ | ☐ |
| 5. author | ☐ | ☐ |
| 6. health | ☐ | ☐ |

**Step Up Note:** *The paragraph in Exercise 8.11 could be the answer to an integrated speaking task on the iBT contrasting different opinions between a reading and a lecture.*

## iBT

## EXERCISE 8.11

1. Read the paragraph, underline all the *th* sounds, and write /ð/ as in *this* or /θ/ as in *thin* above each one.

The author's opinion is that the Earth is getting warmer because of the thinning of the ozone layer. This is thought to be dangerous for health because thermal rays from the sun can reach the Earth, thus causing skin cancer. However, the lecturer thinks that this theory is incorrect. Even though he accepts that the Earth is getting warmer, there have been other periods of increased warmth in history, he says. In 30 years' time, those scientists like him might be thought to be telling the truth.

Track 51. Listen to the audio. Listen to the correct pronunciation. Check your answers.

Practice reading the text with the correct *th* sounds.

## Asking Questions

It is important to recognize questions when you hear them because the iBT listening section could ask you about the function (or, purpose) of part of the dialogue or lecture. Questions can have several functions: to ask for **information,** to ask a student to show knowledge **(display questions),** or to organize a lecture or an answer to an integrating speaking task **(rhetorical questions).** Rhetorical questions don't need an answer: the speaker usually answers the question.

*Which courses are you taking this semester?* → information question

*How many electrons are there in an oxygen atom?* → display question

*Why do some people oppose bilingual education?* → rhetorical question

### Watch Your Step!

Questions have a special word order and intonation:

- *Wh-* word questions have inverted (verb-subject) word order. Intonation rises and falls at the end of the question: *Where is the library?*

- If the *wh-* word is also the subject of the verb, the word order doesn't change: *Who can tell me the answer?*

- Yes/no questions begin with a verb. Inonation rises at the end of the question: *Is there another explanation?*

- In speech, you can also make a question by saying a normal sentence with rising intonation. This is often rhetorical: *So, personality is all genetic? No . . .*

## EXERCISE 8.12

Track 52. Listen to the extracts. Answer the questions about the function of the questions you hear.

1. Why does the advisor ask, "Do you know where that is?"

   a. She can't remember the answer.

   b. She doesn't know where the administration building is.

   c. She is interested in the student's opinion.

   d. She is checking that the student knows this information.

2. Why does the professor ask, "What is capitalism?"

   a. He doesn't know what capitalism is.

   b. He is introducing a new topic.

   c. He wants to hear the students' opinions.

   d. He wants the students to answer his question.

3. Why does the man ask, "When is it due?"

   a. He does not know when the homework is due.

   b. He is making a joke.

   c. He is checking that the woman knows when the homework is due.

   d. He is asking for an opinion.

4. What is the woman's opinion about baby sign language?

   a. She thinks it is a good idea.

   b. She doesn't know what it is.

   c. She believes the argument in the article.

   d. She does not think it is good advice.

5. Why does the professor ask the student these questions?

   a. He is angry with the student.

   b. He wants to know the student's opinion.

   c. He wants to show the student her mistake.

   d. He wants more information about the topic.

### Exercise 8.13

*Make the sentences questions. Use the* wh- *word in parentheses or make a* yes/no *question. The first one has been done for you as an example.*

1. Universities operate like businesses. *(why)*

   <u>Why do universities operate like businesses?</u>

2. Recycling programs save energy. *(yes/no)*

   _____

3. Metals are the best conductors of electricity. *(which)*

   _____

4. Trees help to clean the air. *(how)*

   _____

5. Non-verbal communication is more important than verbal communication. *(yes/no)*

   _____

*Practice saying the questions with the correct intonation.*
*Track 53. Listen to the audio. Listen to the correct question forms. Check your answers.*

> *Step Up Note:* The paragraph in Exercise 8.14 could be the answer to an integrated speaking task on the iBT, summarizing information about conflict. However, you should not use so many rhetorical questions in one answer on the real test!

**iBT**

## EXERCISE 8.14

1.  Read the paragraph, and fill each blank with a rhetorical question. The first one has been done for you as an example. You don't need to understand *contending* and *yielding;* they are defined in the paragraph.

Conflict means a problem or argument between people. <u>How can we resolve a</u> <u>conflict?</u> There are two ways to resolve a conflict: *contending* and *yielding.*

_____

_____

Contending means that a third person makes a decision about how to end the conflict. For example, your parents might tell you and your sister to stop fighting.

_____

_____

No, it doesn't always work because you might both be unhappy with the solution. _____

_____

The other strategy is called *yielding.* Yielding is when you choose to lose the argument. _____
You might do this because you don't want to create a bad feeling with someone.

_____

_____

I don't think there is one right answer: it depends on the conflict.

2.  Practice speaking the paragraph, paying special attention to the intonation of your questions.

3.  Track 54. Listen to the answer. Check your answers and your pronunciation.

# Appendix A: Common Irregular Verbs

| Infinite (Base Form) | Simple Past Tense | Present Participle (Present Perfect Tense) |
|---|---|---|
| be | was / were | been |
| become | became | become |
| begin | began | begun |
| break | broke | broken |
| bring | brought | brought |
| build | built | built |
| buy | bought | bought |
| catch | caught | caught |
| choose | chose | chosen |
| come | came | come |
| cost | cost | cost |
| cut | cut | cut |
| do | did | done |
| draw | drew | drawn |
| drink | drank | drunk |
| drive | drove | driven |
| eat | ate | eaten |
| fall | fell | fallen |
| feel | felt | felt |
| fight | fought | fought |
| find | found | found |
| forget | forgot | forgotten |
| freeze | froze | frozen |
| get | got | [1]gotten |
| give | gave | given |
| go | went | gone |
| grow | grew | grown |
| have | had | had |
| hear | heard | heard |
| hide | hid | hidden |
| hold | held | held |
| hurt | hurt | hurt |
| keep | kept | kept |
| know | knew | known |
| lead | led | led |
| leave | left | left |

[1] The past participle of *get* is *gotten* in North American English but *got* in British English.

| | | |
|---|---|---|
| let | let | let |
| lose | lost | lost |
| make | made | made |
| mean | meant | meant |
| meet | met | met |
| pay | paid | paid |
| put | put | put |
| quit | quit | quit |
| read | read | [2]read |
| ride | rode | ridden |
| ring | rang | rung |
| rise | rose | risen |
| run | ran | run |
| say | said | said |
| see | saw | seen |
| sell | sold | sold |
| send | sent | sent |
| set | set | set |
| shoot | shot | shot |
| show | showed | shown |
| shut | shut | shut |
| sing | sang | sung |
| sit | sat | sat |
| sleep | slept | slept |
| speak | spoke | spoken |
| spend | spent | spent |
| stand | stood | stood |
| steal | stole | stolen |
| swim | swam | swum |
| take | took | taken |
| teach | taught | taught |
| tell | told | told |
| think | thought | thought |
| understand | understood | understood |
| wake | woke | woken |
| wear | wore | worn |
| win | won | won |
| write | wrote | written |

[2] The infinitive *read* is pronounced "reed." The simple past and past participle forms are pronounced "red."

# Appendix B: Contractions

| Be | | | | |
|---|---|---|---|---|
| **Simple Present (Affirmative)** | | **Simple Present (Negative)** | | **Simple Past (Negative)** |
| I am | I'm | I'm not | — | I wasn't |
| You are | You're | You're not | You aren't | You weren't |
| He is | He's | He's not | He isn't | He wasn't |
| She is | She's | She's not | She isn't | She wasn't |
| It is | It's | It's not | It isn't | It wasn't |
| We are | We're | We're not | We aren't | We weren't |
| They are | They're | They're not | They aren't | They weren't |

| Have | | | | |
|---|---|---|---|---|
| **Simple Present (Affirmative)** | | **Simple Present (Negative)** | **Simple Past (Affirmative) (Negative)** | |
| I have | I've | I haven't | I'd | I hadn't |
| You have | You've | You haven't | You'd | You hadn't |
| He has | He's | He hasn't | He'd | He hadn't |
| She has | She's | She hasn't | She'd | She hadn't |
| It has | It's | It hasn't | It'd (*rare) | It hadn't |
| We have | We've | We haven't | We'd | We hadn't |
| They have | They've | They haven't | They'd | They hadn't |

| Other Verbs | |
|---|---|
| I do not sing | I don't sing |
| You did not sing | You didn't sing |
| He does not sing | He doesn't sing |

# Appendix C: Pronouns

| Subject Pronouns | Object Pronouns | Possessive Pronouns |
|---|---|---|
| I | me | my |
| you | you | your |
| he | him | his |
| she | her | her |
| it | it | its |
| we | us | our |
| they | them | their |

# Vocabulary Index

All words are in the top 2,000 most frequent words in English (the General Service List; see To the Teacher, p. x), except:

* = word is on the Academic Word List

† = word is not on the Academic Word List or the General Service List

## Unit 1

academic*
after
assignment*
at 8 AM
at the same time
before
century
character
conversation
crack
day
decade*
dormitory†
drama*
during
earlier
economics*
era†
eventually*
experiment
following
former
freedom
generation*
graduate†
immediately,
immigrant*

in 1587
in the meantime
in the past
in the spring / summer /
    fall / autumn / winter
initially*
last
later
meanwhile
month
native
next
nowadays
on Monday
part
period*
point
predict*
previous, previously*
procedure*
research*
stage
state
step
still
student union
successful
these days
today

tourist
village
week
weekday†
when
while
year

## Unit 2

activity
alike
ancient
both . . . and
chemical*
citizen
consume*
contrast, in contrast to,
    contrasting*
cooperate*
culture*
democracy†
different, difference, differ
digital†
distinction*
gene†
have something in
    common
influenced
not only . . . but also

136

opposite
poverty
powerful
resemble†
salary
semester†
share
similar*
social sciences
surface
technique*
theory*
unlike
values
violence

## Unit 3

ability
advance
advisor†
affect*
another
argue, argument
average
behavior
campus†
challenge*
change
college
course
data*
decline*
decrease
development
discovery
go down
go up
grow

idea
improvement
increase
interpretation*
issue*
lesson
media*
obesity†
other
plan
population
prevent
problem
project*
proposal
reason
reduce
relationship
reliable*
requirement*
resolve*
rise
seminar†
situation
unemployment
valuable
vary*

## Unit 4

accompany*
admissions†
alone
at the same time
ban†
be associated with
be due to
be responsible for
because (of)

bullying†
cause
channel*
childhood
coincidence*
coincidentally*
connection
critic
depression, depressed*
event
fee*
imply*
invention
lead to
link*
ordinary
pollution†
promote*
refuse
region*
reporter
result
so that
technology*
tuition†
wage
war

## Unit 5

answer
apologize
approach*
attitude*
certain
cure
difficulty
distance
extension

face
fair
fix
housing
matter
negative*
positive*
present
problematic
proposal
propose
prove
provider
psychology*
public
reduce
resolution*
respond to, response*
roommate†
settle
settlement
solution
solve
source*
suggest, suggestion
summary, summarize*
tax
trust

## Unit 6

a bit
abroad
actually
agree
almost
announcement†
appointment
avoid

believe
creative*
degree
disagree
disturb
expert*
fortunately
frequently
generally
hopefully†
I guess
illegal*
illness
in general
in my experience
just
kind of
limited
manners
maybe
minor*
nearly
occasionally
often
patient
perhaps
personally
quite
realize
register*
regrettably†
replace
resident*
rude
slightly
sometimes
somewhat*
sort of
suspect

unfortunately
usually

## Unit 7

be known as
central
coal
confidence
definition, define*
efficient
election
environment*
escape
expect
expression
farmer
island
lake
market
mean, meaning
painting
phrase†
protect
relatively
scene
scientific
standard
stands for
sunburn
technical*
temperature
term
transportation*
tribe

# Unit 8

according to

analysis*

announcement†

appearance

application

argue

article

assume*

attendance

author*

bilingual†

book

characteristic

claim

container

crime

criminal

department

discussion

explain

lecture,* lecturer,*

microwave†

nature

notice

nurture†

opinion

passage

personality†

point out

politician

president

professor†

quantity

rate

reading

report

researcher*

review

safety

scientist

speaker

specific*

speech

study

tendency

text*

writer

# Answer Key

## Unit 1: Chronology and Sequences

### Exercise 1.1 (page 3)

1. My <u>favorite</u> place <u>is</u> our basement. My band (is using) it to practice. When (we're playing) our music, my parents <u>don't hear</u> us!

2. Although English <u>is</u> the most widely-spoken language in the U.S., the number of Spanish speakers (is growing) fast.

3. Today, (we're talking) about changes in beliefs about science. (Are you all looking) at page 125 in your textbook?

4. "(I'm taking) Econ 120 this semester, and (I'm looking) for the textbook. Where <u>do you keep</u> the Economics books?"

### Exercise 1.2 (pages 3–4)

1. c   2. a   3. b   4. a   5. d.

### Exercise 1.3 (pages 4–5)

Answers will vary. Sample responses:

1. I like to study in my dorm room.

2. Today, I'm studying in a coffee shop.

3. I usually walk to school.

4. Later today, I'm going shopping with my friend.

5. On Friday, a jazz band is playing a concert.

### Exercise 1.4 (pages 6–7)

1. c   3. e   4. f   6. a.   7. g.   8. d

## Exercise 1.5 (pages 7–8)

2. The professor was going to give a quiz, but she is waiting until next week.

3. The Liberty Bell was a gift from England.

4. When the bell arrived in Philadelphia, a crack appeared.

5. Another crack appeared later when the bell was ringing for Washington's birthday.

6. The governor of Pennsylvania was trying to create a free state.

7. People were coming to America because they wanted freedom of religion.

## Exercise 1.6 (page 9)

1. Previously    2. former    3. decade    4. In    5. period

## Exercise 1.7 (page 9)

1. before

2. before

3. after

4. after

5. after

6. before

7. after

## Exercise 1.8 (pages 10–11)

Answers will vary. Sample responses:
start out / stage / Eventually / Meanwhile / next / final / arrive

## Exercise 1.9 (page 11)

1. b    2. b.    3. c.    4. d.    5. a

## Exercise 1.10 (page 13)

2. <u>She is</u> a great teacher! [She's]

3. <u>You are</u> joking! [You're]

4. Dr. Lin <u>did not</u> give any homework, did he? [didn't]

5. <u>Are you not</u> going to the lab now? [Aren't you]

6. I <u>was not</u> ready for the test. [wasn't]

7. <u>We are</u> on page 57. [We're]

8. The citizens are angry and <u>they are</u> not afraid to fight. [they're]

## Exercise 1.11  (page 13)

| /t/ | /d/ | /ɪd/ |
|---|---|---|
| helped | blamed | interested |
| looked | received | excited |
| passed | allowed | wanted |
| watched | | needed |
| shocked | | |

## Exercise 1.12 (page 14)

                /d/           wasn't              /d/
When I was a child, I play<u>ed</u> the piano. I <u>was not</u> very good, but I enjoy<u>ed</u> the

     I'm                               /d/     /ɪd/
music. <u>I am</u> thinking now about one piece of music that I learn<u>ed</u>. I want<u>ed</u> to play

                 /ɪd/             /t/
it really well, but I need<u>ed</u> more time. I practic<u>ed</u> every day. Finally, in the

            /ɪd/                           wasn't    /d/
concert, I manag<u>ed</u> to play the piece! My teacher said she <u>was not</u> surpris<u>ed</u>.

She's                She's
<u>She is</u> a great piano player. <u>She is</u> always playing difficult music. But I was so

    /ɪd/
excit<u>ed</u>.

# Unit 2: Similarities and Differences

## Exercise 2.1 (page 17)

2. less interesting than

3. as dangerous as

4. more slowly than

5. fewer choices

6. do not consume as much as

## Exercise 2.2 (page 17)

| Film cameras: | 1. more professional photographers<br><br>2. harder to edit |
|---|---|
| Digital cameras: | 1. newer<br><br>2. easier to use<br><br>3. fewer mistakes |

## Exercise 2.3 (page 18)

Answers will vary. Sample responses:

2. Living in a dormitory is cheaper than living in an apartment.

   Living in a dormitory is less private than living in an apartment.

3. Airplanes and trains are faster than cars.

   Airplanes and trains are as comfortable as cars.

4. High school graduates earn less money than college graduates.

   High school graduates get more work experience than college graduates.

5. Life in the 1800s was harder than life today.

   Life in the 1800s was not as complicated as life today.

## Exercise 2.4 (page 20)

2. Coal and diamonds have the same atoms, but they have different structures.

3. Some musicals are sung without any speaking, so they are similar to operas.

4. A volt is a unit of electricity whereas a joule is a unit of energy.

5. Although humans have used language for thousands of years, writing is a more recent invention.

## Exercise 2.5 (page 21)

| Mars: | 1. no water on surface |
| | 2. people cannot breathe |
| | 3. further from the Sun |
| Earth: | 1. more water in atmosphere |
| | 2. warmer |

## Exercise 2.6 (page 23)

1. True     2. False.     3. True.     4. True     5. False

## Exercise 2.7 (page 24)

1. Greece     2. Rome     3. Rome     4. Rome     5. Greece

## Exercise 2.8 (page 25)

Answers will vary. Sample response:

*The Catcher in the Rye* and *The Outsiders* are both books about teenagers. The heroes resemble each other because they are both teenage boys. However, there is a difference between the authors. The author of *The Catcher in the Rye* was an adult unlike the author of *The Outsiders*, who was a teenager. The novels also differ in their endings because *The Outsiders* has a more optimistic ending.

## Exercise 2.9 (page 26)

2. <u>Astronomy</u> is the study of the stars, while <u>astrology</u> means predicting the future.

3. Unlike college <u>basketball</u>, college <u>hockey</u> is not a popular TV sport.

4. I'm interested in the <u>class</u>, but I don't like the <u>professor</u>.

5. So, you're saying that <u>protons</u> have a <u>positive</u> charge, and <u>electrons</u> have a <u>negative</u> charge?

## Exercise 2.10 (page 27)

What are the differences between <u>universities</u> and community <u>colleges</u>? Most people go to a university for <u>four</u> years, but you go to a community college for <u>two</u> years. Universities are also very <u>expensive</u>, but community colleges are <u>cheaper</u>. Also, you can be in a <u>large</u> class at a university, but a <u>small</u> class at a community college. Universities are mostly <u>academic</u>, unlike community colleges, which are often <u>vocational</u>.

## Exercise 2.11 (page 28)

LIST 2. a. water  b. unit  c. different  d. listen  e. resemble

## Exercise 2.12 (page 28)

Answers will vary. Sample responses that can serve as models follow.

1. second grade

   English teacher

   Mrs. Head

   used a green pen to correct our writing

   taught us to use strong words not weak words

   write novels when grew up

2. Words to stess: *second, Head, green, strong, weak, novels*

   Reduced vowels: second, correct, novels

3. My second-grade English teacher was a woman called Mrs. Head. She was very important to me because she was the first teacher who helped me to like writing. Most teachers used red pens, but Mrs. Head used a green pen to correct our writing. She gave me many useful comments. She always taught us to use strong words, not weak words like *nice, good,* and *bad.* I liked writing so much that I wanted to write novels when I grew up!

# Unit 3: Developing Ideas

## Exercise 3.1 (page 31)

2. Children are born with the ability to speak any language, but they only actually learn the language of their environment.

3. Darwin began to think about evolution on his voyage to the Galapagos Islands.

4. The Americans with Disabilities Act guarantees disabled people their basic human rights.

5. Although they are not accepted by many Western doctors, some herbs are often used as medications in the East.

## Exercise 3.2 (page 31)

2. They    3. He    4. their    5. me    6. it

## Exercise 3.3 (pages 32–33)

1. a    2. c    3. c    4. b    5. a    6. c

## Exercise 3.4 (page 35)

Answers will vary. Sample responses:

2. The conductor helps the orchestra keep time. In addition, he or she decides the mood and interpretation of the music.

3. Some bacteria cause illnesses in the human body. On the other hand, other types of bacteria are important for health.

4. The Great Lakes are a valuable source of fish. Furthermore. they are an essential means of transportation.

5. Chimpanzees can produce some kinds of language. However, they cannot produce the same range of expression as humans.

## Exercise 3.5 (page 35)

1. Use     2. Use     3. Use     4. Don't use

## Exercise 3.6 (page 36)

Answers will vary. Sample responses:

2. Some parents are not kind to their children. However, these parents are not the best teachers. Therefore, children need other teachers.

3. Children learn good behavior from their parents. They also learn bad behavior. For example, sometimes parents argue in front of their children. As a result, these children do not grow up to be polite.

4. Parents can teach their children a lot. On the other hand, young people learn more from their friends. For instance, they learn how to play on a team. In addition, they learn how to resolve an argument.

## Exercise 3.7 (page 38)

Culture shock is the uncomfortable feeling you have when you live for a time in a different country. This feeling is normal, but you can reduce the effects of culture shock. These actions sound simple, but they are very effective. / The first thing you can do is keep contact with friends and family at home. / Another idea is to join a club, society, or religious organization. This will give you some support in the new country. / A further solution is physical exercise. Some people find this very helpful when they are frustrated.

## Exercise 3.8 (page 38)

2. idea

3. Another

4. This

5. improvement

## Exercise 3.9 (page 39)

1. class — lesson — course — seminar

2. school — college — university — academic

3. question — issue — problem — challenge

4. increase — rise — grow — go up

5. decrease — decline — go down — reduce

6. plan — project — idea — proposal

7. progress — advance — improvement — development

## Exercise 3.10 (pages 40–41)

1. c     2. c     3. d     4.b     5. a

## Exercise 3.11 (page 42)

In today's lecture / I'm going to talk about / English theater / in the late 16<sup>th</sup> century. The most famous writer, of course / was William Shakespeare, / but he had a lot of competition. The most popular play of the 1580s / for example / was called / *The Spanish Tragedy* / by Thomas Kyd. We don't know exactly / when it was performed, / but it was probably first acted / in London / in the 1580s.

## Exercise 3.12 (page 43)

Answers will vary.

## Exercise 3.13 (page 44)

*Student:*  I have a <u>question</u> / about my <u>classes</u>.

*Advisor:*  What's your <u>major</u>?

*Student:*  I'm a <u>business</u> major, /  but I have to take a <u>writing</u> class.

*Advisor:*  <u>Everyone</u> has to do that!

*Student:* I <u>understand</u>. / I'm interested in <u>history</u>,/ so I <u>want</u> to take / a history <u>composition</u> class.

*Advisor:* That's <u>possible</u>. / Next <u>semester</u>, / there's a class on <u>American</u> history.

*Student:* But the class is <u>full</u>!

*Advisor:* Let me call the <u>department</u>. / If you're <u>lucky</u>, / they'll say <u>yes.</u>

# Unit 4: Cause, Effect, and Correlation

## Exercise 4.1 (page 47)

1. have lived    2. hit    3. has changed    4. have risen    5. have gone

## Exercise 4.2 (pages 47–48)

1. b    2. d    3. c    4.

| TV journalists | 1. We know more about wars. |
|---|---|
| Some critics of television | 1. We are not interested in wars. <br> 2. Wars do not shock us. |

## Exercise 4.3 (page 50)

2. is going to grow / will grow

3. are smoking / will smoke

4. decreases

5. learn

## Exercise 4.4 (pages 50–51)

Answers will vary. Sample responses:

2. I'd prefer a job that I enjoy. If I have a high-salary job I don't enjoy, I won't enjoy the extra money. However, I am also not going to take a fun job that I can't live off.

3. The population is going to increase in the next decade. Therefore, there won't be enough food and resources for the world. This will cause wars because some countries aren't going to have access to fresh water.

4. No, I don't agree with this statement. I think it is true that English, Chinese, and Spanish will become languages of international communication, but native languages will survive, especially in poorer regions where fewer people can travel.

## Exercise 4.5 (pages 51–52)

1. b    2. c    3. d    4. c    5. a

6. Answers will vary. Sample response:

The man thinks that it is a bad idea to charge all students to use the university gym. He says that he never uses the gym, so he should not have to pay for it. He thinks that the students who use the gym should pay the new fee.

## Exercise 4.6 (page 54)

2. Due to the <u>public holiday,</u> <sub>C</sub> <u>classes are cancelled</u> <sub>E</sub> on Monday.

          C                      E
2. Due to the <u>public holiday,</u> <u>classes are cancelled</u> on Monday.

         C                            E
3. <u>The election</u> resulted in <u>a clear win for the President.</u>

              E                         C
4. <u>The student is unhappy</u> because of her <u>grade.</u>

          C                            E
5. <u>Eating fruits and vegetables</u> promotes <u>good health.</u>

## Exercise 4.7 (pages 54–55)

1. d    2. c    3. b    4. d    5. a

## Exercise 4.8 (page 55)

Answers will vary. Sample responses:

2. All children should play a sport since an active lifestyle promotes good health.

3. In the past, doctor did not know that germs causes disease. As a result, some germs caused many deaths.

4. I think zoos are bad animals. Zoos are responsible for animals behaving strangely, which can lead to illness for the animals.

5. Economics should be a required subject for all high-school students so that they will know how to manage their money when they are older.

## Exercise 4.9 (page 57)

1. c    2. b    3. a    4. d    5. d

## Exercise 4.10 (page 59)

          **gonna**          **otta**

Teenagers aren't <u>going to</u> listen to doctors, so the government <u>ought to</u> use the

          **gonna**

Internet. If kids see a really good website about obesity, they're <u>going to</u> read it.

          **wanna**

An even better idea is to use an Internet video. Teenagers <u>want to</u> watch what

          **gonna**

their friends are watching, so the video's <u>going to</u> spread quickly. This shows

          **havta**

that modern problems <u>have to</u> have modern solutions.

# Unit 5: Problems and Solutions

## Exercise 5.1 (page 63)

Answers will vary. Sample responses:

2. A tax cut can improve the quality of life.

3. Researcher might find a cure for cancer in the next 15 years.

4. According to historians, Arthur could be a real British king / could have been a real British king.

5. The experiment might prove Darwin's theory of evolution.

## Exercise 5.2 (page 64)

1. a. author   b. professor   c. author   d. professor   e. professor   f. author

2. Answers will vary. Sample response:

> I agree with the author of the article but for different reasons. TV news broadcasts could end because people may not trust TV journalists. Young people might prefer to get their news from many online sources. We can see this change already today. If TV channels do not get enough viewers, they could stop showing the news. Then, people who can't access the Internet might have to listen to the radio or buy newspapers.

## Exercise 5.3 (pages 66–67)

1. d     2. c     3. d     4. b     5. a     6. c

## Exercise 5.4 (page 68)

1. d     2. b     3. d     4. a     5. d

## Exercises 5.5 (page 70)

Answers will vary. Sample responses:

problem / challenge / issue / problematic / difficulty / challenging

## Exercise 5.6 (page 70)

Answers will vary. Sample response:

> The woman is having a problem with her group project for Dr. Webber's class. One member of her group is being difficult. One challenge is that he never finds time to meet with the group. Another difficulty is his opinions, which are different from the rest of the group. This student presents a real problem for her, and she is worried that her group will have difficulty finishing their project.

# Exercise 5.7 (page 72)

Answers will vary. Sample responses:

2. I could respond to their objection by getting a part-time job to earn money for my trip. Another suggestion is to do volunteer work on my trip.

3. We could settle this problem if my roommate wears headphones. I could resolve the issue by working in the library.

4. We can solve this problem by taking public transportation. Another fix is to encourage people to walk to work.

5. The school can respond with a fashionable uniform. The students might settle for a uniform they like.

# Exercise 5.8 (page 73)

Answers will vary. Samples responses:

1. Shellshock was a major challenge for soldiers after World War I. Daily life presented a problem for them because of this emotional difficulty.

2. Freud responded to shellshock with a treatment called the talking cure. He thought that soldiers were probably reliving their experiences. When soldiers talked about the war, Freud could fix their shellshock.

3. A big difficulty for soldiers after World War I was shellshock. Shellshock is an emotional problem. Daily life was difficult for the soldiers. Sigmund Freud suggested an answer to this problem with the talking cure. If the soldiers talked about their war experiences, they might resolve them and settle their shellshock.

# Exercise 5.9 (page 74)

Answers will vary. Sample responses:

1. The final exam in Professor James's class is on the same day as her grandmother's 90th birthday.

2. a. not take the final; get worse grade

   b. take the exam before going home

   c. write an essay

3. I chose solution (c). This is the best resolution because there is no extra work for the professor, it is fair to the other students, and she can go home without lowering her grade.

4. The student is worried about her final exam in Professor James' class. The exam is on the same day as her grandmother's 90th birthday. She can resolve this problem and still go home for her grandmother's birthday. She could propose this solution to her professor: she will write an essay instead of taking the final exam. This is a good resolution because she can show her knowledge in the essay, but the professor does not have to work harder and write a different exam for her. An essay might be harder than the final, so it is fair for her and her classmates.

## Exercise 5.10 (page 75)

1. can

2. can't

3. can

4. can't

5. can

## Exercise 5.11 (page 76)

1. True

2. False

3. True

4. True

5. True

6. False

## Exercise 5.12 (page 77)

2. There are three solutions to this problem: increase education, lower the requirements, or employ foreign workers.

3. Nuclear energy presents three major challenges: storing the waste product, securing the power plants, and protecting the population.

4. Salary, discipline, and testing are the three biggest problems for today's teachers.

5. A business can fail in many ways—it can choose the wrong location, it can set its prices badly, it can hire the wrong people, and it can promote itself poorly.

## Exercise 5.13 (page 77)

Answers will vary. Sample response:

1. Languages change for three reasons: contact with other languages, the need for new words, and internal change.

# Unit 6: Preferences and Opinions

## Exercise 6.1 (page 80)

Answers will vary. Suggested responses:

1. need to

2. are supposed to

3. have to

4. should

5. don't have to

## Exercise 6.2 (page 81)

| Necessary: | 1. balance the foods we eat |
| | 2. calcium |
| | 3. exercise |
| Recommended or optional: | 1. whole grains |
| | 2. drink milk |

## Exercise 6.3 (page 82)

1. d     2. c     3. c     4. b

## Exercise 6.4 (pages 84–85)

1. d     2. d     3. b     4. a     5. d

## Exercise 6.5 (page 85)

Answer will vary. Sample responses:

2. If you need an immediate response from someone, IM is faster than email.

3. I had to ask them when I wanted to go to my friend's house.

4. If fewer people buy music legally, the cost of CDs and MP3s will go up.

5. When you live in a dorm, you can meet more people.

## Exercise 6.6 (page 87)

1. a. direct grammar

   b. direct grammar

   c. communicative language teaching

   d. communicative language teaching

2. c     3. d     4. a

## Exercise 6.7 (page 88)

Answers will vary. Sample responses:

1. I believe that smoking is bad, and personally, I believe people should not smoke anywhere. However, I have realized that a law against smoking is a bad idea. I suggest that it is better to teach people about the dangers of smoking.

2. I disagree with this statement. I believe that parents can teach their children a lot, for example, good manners. However, in my experience, children learn more from their peers at school because they have to use good social skills.

3. I agree with this statement. Unfortunately, if people live too close together, they often have arguments. I have realized that we all need some private space. If we respect each other's fences, I believe we can all live together more peacefully.

4. I agree with this idea. Regrettably, I suspect universities and employers look first at your high school scores. Therefore, I suggest that high schools teach students to pass tests, and also to be good people.

5. Personally, I am not very good at sports, so I agree with this idea. I don't like to lose, but I have realized that I can enjoy a good game even if I don't win.

## Exercise 6.8 (page 90)

2. ✔ a. (Generally,) pop music has (slightly) simpler melodies than classical music.

3. ✔ b. (Most) people believe that (few) animals can learn to speak.

4. ✔ b. "(Actually,) the admissions secretary is (kind of) rude."

5. ✔ b. "Jim is failing the class. (I guess) he's (just) (sort of) lazy."

## Exercise 6.9 (page 91)

Answers will vary. Sample response:

Technology might improve classroom learning. Computers can help some students improve some of their language skills. Generally, learners are somewhat more interested in the class when the teacher uses technology. We could actually do many class activities on computers. Furthermore, the Internet can be useful for certain homework assignments. In conclusion, perhaps we might replace some textbooks with technology.

## Exercise 6.10 (pages 91–92)

1. a     2. d     3. b     4. a     5. c

## Exercise 6.11 (page 93)

1. b     2. a     3. c     4. a     5. c

## Exercise 6.12 (page 93)

Answers will vary.

## Exercise 6.13 (page 95)

| | |
|---|---|
| *Student (F):* | <u>Uh</u> . . . hi. I have a question about my tuition fees. |
| *Secretary (M):* | I'm sorry, we don't answer questions in person. |
| *F:* | <u>Oh</u>, I see. <u>Well</u>, how can I ask my question, then? |
| *M:* | You need to send us an email, and we'll back to you in, <u>uh</u>, 48 hours. |
| *F:* | <u>Ah</u>, that's a problem. The bill is due tomorrow and I think there's been a mistake. |
| *M:* | <u>Well</u>, all right. I'll take a look at it. <u>Oh no</u>, that's not right. It should be $100 not $1000. |
| *F:* | <u>Wow!</u> That's a big difference. |

## Exercise 6.14 (page 95)

Answers will vary.

# Unit 7: Paraphrasing

## Exercise 7.1 (page 98)

2. I was born in a small town that (or which) is famous for its cheese.

3. The tree that (or which) was used to build canoes was the birch tree.

4. A National Park is an area of natural beauty that (or which) is protected by the government.

5. The Ojibwe are a Native American tribe who live in the Midwest and Canada.

## Exercise 7.2 (pages 98–99)

2. Snowshoes, which are a cross between a shoe and a ski, were an important means of transportation.

3. Some farmers who began to rotate their crops were more successful.

4. Edison made nearly one hundred designs for a light bulb that (or which) didn't work.

5. S. E. Hinton, who is a very successful author, got poor grades for creative writing in high school.

6. The CPU, which stands for central processing unit, is the brain of a computer.

## Exercise 7.3 (page 99)

Answers will vary. Sample responses:

2. Calcium is a mineral that (or which) keeps your bones strong.

3. A pixel is a measurement that (or which) is equal to one dot on a computer screen or printer.

4. An archeologist is a person who studies old cultures.

5. A peninsula is a piece of land that (or which) is surrounded on all sides by water.

## Exercise 7.4 (page 100)

Answers will vary. Sample response:

Mackinac Island, which <u>is located between Lake Michigan and Lake Huron</u>, attracts a lot of tourists. Because there are no cars, tourists use other types of transportation, which <u>include bikes and horses</u>. A ferry, which <u>runs from May to October</u>, takes tourists to the island. However, people who <u>live on the island in winter</u> have to fly.

## Exercise 7.5 (pages 100–101)

1. b    2. d    3. a    4. b    5. c    6. a

## Exercise 7.6 (page 103)

2. are

3. is rising

4. are

5. can not / cannot / can't

6. does not pass / doesn't pass

## Exercise 7.7 (page 103)

Answers will vary. Sample responses:

1. Skin becomes darker when <u>it is out in the sun.</u>

2. People can get sunburn if <u>they are in the sun for a long time.</u>

3. The SPF, or sun protection factor, <u>is a number that tells you the strength of suntan lotion.</u>

4. A suntan lotion with a high SPF <u>means you can stay in the sun for longer without getting sunburn.</u>

## Exercise 7.8 (page 104)

2. Filmmakers (call) <u>the scenes that they film in one day</u> the *dailies.*

3. Digital camera lenses are measured in how many <u>thousands of tiny dots they record,</u> (or) megapixels.

4. ABS, (which stands for) <u>anti-lock braking system</u>, is standard in most new cars.

5. (The meaning of) hubris for the ancient Greeks was <u>extreme pride and confidence in human ability.</u>

## Exercise 7.9 (page 105)

Answers will vary. Sample responses:

2. The scenes that film-makers film in one day are known as the "dailies."

3. Digital camera lenses are measured in megapixels, which means how many thousands of tiny dots they record.

4. ABS, or anti-lock braking system, is standard in most new cars.

5. The Greeks defined *hubris* as "extreme pride and confidence in human ability."

## Exercise 7.10 (pages 105–6)

1.

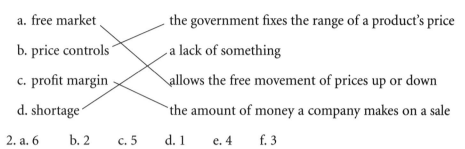

a. free market          the government fixes the range of a product's price

b. price controls          a lack of something

c. profit margin          allows the free movement of prices up or down

d. shortage          the amount of money a company makes on a sale

2. a. 6     b. 2     c. 5     d. 1     e. 4     f. 3

3. Answers will vary. Sample response:

Experts define a free market as an economy that allows the free movement of prices. However, some governments use price control when a product becomes too expensive for customers. Price control means that the government fixes the range of a product's price. As a result, the profit margin, or the amount of money a company makes on the sale of this product, becomes smaller. Then the companies might stop making the product. This leads to a shortage, which means a lack of the product, and the price of the product will go up.

## Exercise 7.11 (pages 108–9)

Answers will vary. Sample responses:

1. reduce energy 3 ways

   a. old light bulbs → compact fluorescent light bulbs (more efficient, less electricity, last longer)

   b. replace windows with special glass (keeps heat in house)

   c. install solar panels (Definition: devices that convert sun's energy → electricity)

   Save energy = save money + save earth

2. replace = swap; use = consume; way = method; install = put in; convert = change; power your home = generate electricity; save the Earth = be environmentally friendly

3. There are three good methods for lowering your electricity bill. First, <u>swap inefficient light bulbs for new compact fluorescent bulbs</u> because <u>they consume less energy and have a longer life</u>. Second, <u>fit windows</u> with a glass that does not let heat escape. Third, <u>put in</u> solar panels, which <u>generate electricity for your house from the sun</u>. If you use less energy, <u>you will spend less money and be more environmentally friendly</u>.

## Exercise 7.12 (page 109)

Answers will vary. Sample response:

Voting is important for college students because they can show their views in the election. There are three ways to vote. First, students can sign up in advance to vote in their college town. On the day of the election, they have to go to the polling place. The second way is mailing in a voting form, which the student has to ask for before the election. The final method is a proxy vote. Voters allow someone else to cast the vote in their place. Students can vote in three ways, but they should vote.

## Exercise 7.13 (page 111)

2. Britain, / <u>which had controlled America</u>, / went to war as a result.

3. An army leader, / <u>who was called George Washington</u>, / became the first president.

4. There were still people who wanted to be part of Britain.

5. The Americans won the war, / which is known today as the War of Independence.

## Exercise 7.14 (page 112)

Answers will vary. Sample responses:

2. skiing, which is a winter sport

    skis, which are long wooden boards

    piste, which is a slope or run

    meet other people who like skiing

3. Guy Fawkes Day—remember Guy Fawkes, who was a 17th-century protestor

    leader of a group of people who wanted to kill the king

    light bonfires, which are big public fires

    eat toffee apples, which are apples covered with caramel

    enjoy a firework display that the city organizes

## Exercise 7.15 (page 113)

| /s/ | /z/ | / ɪz/ |
|---|---|---|
| eats | reads | watches |
| books | goes | chooses |
| wakes | has | advises |
| writes | rides | |
| | studies | |
| | says | |
| | tells | |

1. /z/    2. /s/    3. / ɪz /

## Exercise 7.16 (page 114)

               /z/                   / ɪz/   /z/      /z/     /z/     /z/

The professor explains that he often catches colds on airplanes. He says that germs

             / ɪz/                     /z/

in the air spread diseases. However, the author disagrees with this opinion. He

 /z/        /s/                   /s/     /z/

argues that no-one gets sick from air travel. The research supports his claims.

# Chapter 8: Sources of Information

## Exercise 8.1 (page 117)

Answers will vary. Sample responses:

2. The reading explains that the university is changing its attendance policy.

3. The professor said that she was going to talk about modern art.

4. The author wrote that acidity is measured on the pH scale.

5. The lecturer reminded us that Washington was the first U.S. president.

6. I told my friend that I would meet him at the library.

## Exercise 8.2 (page 118)

Answers will vary. Sample responses:

| Reading: | 1. The author wrote that single-sex schools have higher test scores. |
| | 2. He explained that girls got better scores in math and science. |
| Lecture: | 1. The professor said that girls are less nervous in mixed schools. |
| | 2. He added that boys feel more motivated in mixed schools. |

## Exercise 8.3 (page 120)

2. Jane's roommate is a history major.

3. Tonight's homework is on page 36.

4. The professor gives her opinion about animal testing.

5. In the words of the current university president, we need a "global focus."

## Exercise 8.4 (page 120)

2. yesterday's newspaper

3. analysis of the data

4. his/her office hours

5. Shakespeare's theater

# Exercise 8.5 (page 121)

Answers will vary. Sample responses:

2. book

3. text

4. experts

5. author

# Exercise 8.6 (page 122)

1. textbook

2. lecturer

3. experts/research

4. textbook

5. experts/research

6. lecturer

# Exercise 8.7 (page 122)

Answers will vary. Sample response:

Hey, Sam! Did you see the notice on the bulletin board this morning? The notice says that there's going to be a class in American Sign Language next semester. It sounds cool. The professor says that it's a really interesting language. And it can help you get a job—that's what the Career Services wrote. I'm going to go online to register this evening.

# Exercise 8.8 (page 123)

Answers will vary. Sample responses:

1. assume

2. argues

3. According

4. proves

5. opinion

## Exercise 8.9 (pages 124–26)

Answers will vary. Sample responses:

1. a. decides our personality as well as our physical characteristics

   b. shy or confident

   c. is also controlled by genes

   d. there is a gene which suggests a person may become a criminal

2. a. The professor agrees that

   b. He argues that

   c. He points out that

   d. According to research,

   e. The professor's opinion is that

3.

| Question 1 | Question 2 |
|------------|------------|
| a.         | a.         |
| b. ——————— | b.         |
| c. ——————— | c.         |
| d. ——————— | d.         |
|            | e.         |

4. The professor agrees with the textbook that DNA decides our physical characteristics, but he does not agree that it also controls our personality. The reading claims that being shy or outgoing is a result of genes. However, the professor argues that children cannot be outgoing without their parents' love when they are very young. The text also claims that playing a musical instrument well is genetic. The lecturer points out that you need to practice the piano even if you have a musical gene. Finally, the textbook asserts that according to research, there is a gene for criminal behavior. However, the speaker disagrees with the study because not all children with the criminal gene grow up to commit crimes. He argues that personality is controlled by nature and nurture together.

## Exercise 8.10 (page 127)

1. δ    2. θ    3. δ    4. δ    5. θ    6. θ

# Exercise 8.11 (page 127)

<pre>
        θ            δ  δ    θ                        δ
The author's opinion is that the Earth is getting warmer because of the

θ        δ            δ    θ                        θ
thinning of the ozone layer. This is thought to be dangerous for health

        θ            δ            δ    θ δ
because thermal rays from the sun can reach the Earth, thus causing skin

        δ            θ    δ  δ    θ
cancer. However, the lecturer thinks that this theory is incorrect. Even

δ                δ  δ    θ            δ            δ
though he accepts that the Earth is getting warmer, there have been other

                θ                θ            δ
periods of increased warmth in history, he says. In thirty years' time, those

                θ                    θ
scientists like him might be thought to be telling the truth.
</pre>

# Exercise 8.12 (page 129)

1. d     2. b     3. a     4. d     5. c

# Exercise 8.13 (page 130)

2. Do recycling programs save energy?

3. Which metals are the best conductors of electricity?

4. How do trees help to clean the air?

5. Is non-verbal communication more important than verbal communication?

# Exercise 8.14 (page 131)

1. What is contending?

   Does it work?

   What is the second strategy?

   Why might you do this?

   So, one strategy is better than the other?

# Audio Transcripts

## Unit 1: Chronology and Sequences

### Exercise 1.2 (pages 3–4). (Track 2)

Listen to the conversation between two students about their study habits.

*M:* Are you going to the library?

*F:* Actually, I'm going to the coffee shop at the student union.

*M:* Oh, I thought you always study in the library.

*F:* That's right, but I'm working on a group project for my biology class. We prefer to meet in the coffee shop.

*M:* I don't like coffee shops—they're too noisy, and the coffee smells too strong.

*F:* So, where do you study?

*M:* Usually, I stay in my dorm room, but today I'm going to the library. I'm doing research for my history class. Normally, I do my research on the Internet, but I need some books for this paper.

### Exercise 1.2, Question 4 (page 4). (Track 3)

Listen again to part of the conversation.

*F:* So, where do you study?

*M:* Usually, I stay in my dorm room, but today I'm going to the library. I'm doing research for my history class.

### Exercise 1.5 (pages 7–8). (Track 4)

Listen to the beginning of a class on American history.

*Professor (F):* OK, everyone. Let's get started. Where did we finish the last class?

*Student (M):* You were telling us about the Liberty Bell in Philadelphia.

*F:* Oh, that's right. I was going to give you a quiz today, but I think I'm going to wait until next week. Did you all read Chapter 3 in the textbook? Good. So, what did you learn about the Liberty Bell?

*M:* It was a gift from England. I didn't know that.

*F:* Yes, it was. But that was before the American Revolution. When the bell arrived in Philadelphia, a crack appeared—the bell was broken. Two craftsmen in Philadelphia remade the bell, but another crack appeared in 1846  while it was ringing for George Washington's birthday. So, why was it called the Liberty Bell?

M:       Liberty means freedom?

F:       Correct. In 1756, when the first governor of Pennsylvania ordered the bell, he was trying to create a free state. People were coming to America because they wanted freedom of religion. So, the governor had the word *liberty* written on the bell.

## Exercise 1.9 (page 11). (Track 5)

Listen to the lecture about immigrants' language patterns.

*Professor (M):* Most immigrant groups to the United States in the nineteenth and early twentieth centuries followed a similar pattern of language use. Initially, the first generation—that is, the first people to move to the United States from their home countries—the first generation just spoke their first language with maybe a bit of English. The second generation—the children of these immigrants—were usually bilingual; they could speak both their parents' language and English fluently. Remember that the children were speaking their mother tongue at home and, at the same time, they were using English at school and with their  friends. In the next stage, the third generation mostly spoke only English. Eventually, though, we see a new development. Later generations want to go back and learn the language of their immigrant ancestors. We call these *heritage language learners.*

## Exercise 1.9, Question 4 (page 11). (Track 6)

Listen again to part of the lecture.

*Professor (M):* Eventually, though, we see a new development. Later generations want to go back and learn the language of their immigrant ancestors. We call these *heritage language learners.*

## Exercise 1.10 (page 13). (Track 7)

Listen to the sentences.

1. I'm looking for the admissions building.

2. She's a great teacher!

3. You're joking!

4. Dr. Lin didn't give any homework, did he?

5. Aren't you going to the lab now?

6. I wasn't ready for the test.

7. We're on page 57.

8. The citizens are angry, and they're not afraid to fight.

## Exercise 1.11 (page 13). (Track 8)

Listen to the words.

| | | |
|---|---|---|
| helped | blamed | interested |
| excited | looked | passed |
| wanted | shocked | allowed |
| received | watched | needed |

## Exercise 1.12 (page 14). (Track 9)

Listen to the answer to this prompt: Describe a memory of a successful learning experience.

When I was a child, I played the piano. I wasn't very good, but I enjoyed the music. I'm thinking now about one piece of music that I learned. I wanted to play it really well, but I needed more time. I practiced every day. Finally, in the concert, I managed to play the piece! My teacher said she wasn't surprised. She's a great piano player. She's always playing difficult music. But I was so excited.

# Unit 2: Similarities and Differences

## Exercise 2.2 (page 17). (Track 10)

Listen to the lecture about photography.

There are a lot of important differences between film cameras and digital cameras. Digital cameras are of course newer than film cameras. There are fewer professional photographers using digital than film. However, digital cameras are as popular as film for most amateurs. Digital cameras are easier than film cameras because you can see the picture immediately, so you don't make as many mistakes with a digital camera. Finally, you can edit digital pictures more easily than traditional photographs.

## Exercise 2.6 (page 23). (Track 11)

Listen to the first part of the lecture about two cultures.

In many ways, the cultures of Ancient Greece and the Roman Empire were very similar. For example, Roman religion was similar to Greek religion. There were many gods, and the Roman gods resembled the Greeks'. Both cultures shared a love of the arts. They also had an idea of government in common—the people, not kings or queens, should make decisions for themselves.

## Exercise 2.7 (page 24). (Track 12)

Listen to the second part of the lecture about Greece and Rome.

But there were also many differences between Ancient Greece and the Roman Empire. In Athens in Greece, for example, democracy differed from Roman government. In Athens, every citizen voted for every decision—in contrast to Rome, where an emperor made many decisions. The two cultures also differed in language, and so the names of their gods were different. For example, Mars is the Roman god of war, whereas the Greek god was called Ares. Another distinction between Greece and Rome was power: the Roman Empire was much more powerful than any city in Greece. Also, unlike Greece, Rome changed its religion to Christianity.

## Exercise 2.9 (page 26). (Track 13) (See also Key page 145).

Listen to the sentences.

1. Trains are fast, but airplanes are faster.

2. Astronomy is the study of the stars, while astrology means predicting the future.

3. Unlike basketball, hockey is not a popular TV sport.

4. I'm interested in the class, but I don't like the professor.

5. So, you're saying that protons have a positive charge, and electrons have a negative charge?

## Exercise 2.10 (page 27). (Track 14) (See also Key page 145).

Listen to the answer to this prompt: What are the differences between universities and community colleges?

Most people go to a university for four years, but you go to a community college for two years. Universities are also very expensive, but community colleges are cheaper. Also, you can be in a large class at a university, but a small class at a community college. Universities are mostly academic, unlike community colleges, which are often vocational.

## Exercise 2.11 (page 28). (Track 15)

Listen to the two lists of words.

| LIST 1. a. pizza | b. college | c. teacher | d. vowel | e. similar |
| LIST 2. a. water | b. unit | c. different | d. listen | e. resemble |

# Unit 3: Developing Ideas

## Exercise 3.5 (page 35). (Track 16)

Listen to the conversation during a professor's office hours about the requirements for a linguistics class.

*Student (F):*   Sorry to bother you, Professor Reed. Could I ask you a question?

*Professor (M):* Sure, Jayne. What can I do for you?

*F:*            I don't understand the requirements for the research paper. Could you explain them again?

| | |
|---|---|
| *M:* | Of course. I want you to find three library sources. Additionally, you need to collect some kind of field data. |
| *F:* | For example, I could tape-record my two-year-old niece? |
| *M:* | Exactly. However, you can't use Internet sources. |

## Exercise 3.11 (page 42). (Track 17) (See also Key page 148).

Listen to the introduction to a lecture about English theater in the 16th century.

In today's lecture I'm going to talk about English theater in the late 16th century. The most famous writer, of course, was William Shakespeare, but he had a lot of competition. The most popular play of the 1580s for example was called *The Spanish Tragedy* by Thomas Kyd. We don't know exactly when it was performed, but it was probably first acted in London in the 1580s.

## Exercise 3.13 (page 44). (Track 18) (See also Key pages 148–49).

Listen to the conversation.

| | |
|---|---|
| *Student (M):* | I have a question about my classes. |
| *Advisor (F):* | What's your major? |
| *(M):* | I'm a business major, but I have to take a writing class. |
| *(F):* | Everyone has to do that! |
| *(M):* | I understand. I'm interested in history, so I want to take a history composition class. |
| *(F):* | That's possible. Next semester, there's a class on American history. |
| *(M):* | But the class is full! |
| *(F):* | Let me call the department. If you're lucky, they'll say yes. |

## Unit 4: Cause, Effect, and Correlation

### Exercise 4.5 (pages 51–52). (Track 19)

Listen to two students discussing the newspaper article.

| | |
|---|---|
| *Student (M):* | Have you seen this article about charging for the gym? |
| *Student (F):* | Yes, we're all going to pay to use the gym. |
| M: | But I never go to the gym. I won't pay. I will refuse to pay the gym fee. |
| F: | That's not fair! If you don't pay, the fee will be higher for the rest of us! |
| M: | That's fine. If you use the gym, you should pay for it. I'm not going to use the gym next semester, so I'm not paying for it. |
| F: | What are you going to do? |
| M: | I'm writing to the university president this afternoon! I'm going to tell her to cancel this charge! |

### Exercise 4.5, Question 4 (page 52). (Track 20)

Listen again to part of the conversation.

M: But I never go to the gym. I won't pay. I will refuse to pay the gym fee.

F: That's not fair! If you don't pay, the fee will be higher for the rest of us!

### Exercise 4.7 (pages 54–55). (Track 21)

Listen to the lecture about teenage depression.

So, what causes depression in teenagers? Well, one reason that teenagers get depressed is stress. For example, when parents push their teenagers too hard to improve their grades, this can promote stress. And stress leads to depression if the teenager doesn't know how to manage it. University admissions are also responsible for depression. Because many good universities are very competitive, students can become depressed when they are not accepted. Relationship problems can also lead to depression, and depression can result in suicide. Consequently, it is important for teenagers to have someone to talk to about their problems.

## Exercise 4.10 (page 59). (Track 22)

Listen to the answer.

Teenagers aren't gonna listen to doctors, so the government ought to use the Internet. If kids see a really good website about obesity, they're gonna read it. An even better idea is to use an Internet video. Teenagers wanna watch what their friends are watching, so the video's gonna spread quickly. This shows that modern problems have to have modern solutions.

## Exercise 4.11 (page 60). (Track 23)

Listen to the sentences.

1. He's asking hard questions.

2. I didn't hear the end of your sentence.

3. Go on to the next page.

4. The water heats up.

5. I'm making a solution.

6. She opens the box.

# Unit 5: Problems and Solutions

## Exercise 5.2 (page 64). (Track 24)

Listen to the conversation between a student and his professor.

*Student (M):* I'm sorry to bother you, Professor, but I have a question about this week's reading.

*Professor (F):* Sit down. I thought you might find it surprising.

*M:* Absolutely! I was confused by this section. He writes: "Television news is not important, and TV networks will stop showing the news. The Internet is the most important source of news today." Is that true?

*F:* Well, it *is* the author's opinion, and he could be right. The Internet may be the most important source of news for some people. But television news could still continue.

*M:* How?

| | |
|---|---|
| *F:* | I think a lot of people don't trust the Internet. In the opinion of this author, everyone will learn to trust websites and blogs. However, that may not be the end of TV news—television news broadcasts could attract a different audience. |
| *M:* | You mean people who might not have an Internet connection? |
| *F:* | Certainly. We sometimes forget how many people do not have access to the Internet. At present, 65 million adult Americans do not use the web. |
| *M:* | It says here in the article that those people could all be online in 5 years. |
| *F:* | What do you think about that? Could he be right? |

## Exercise 5.4 (page 68). (Track 25)

Listen to the conversation between a student and a housing office assistant.

| | |
|---|---|
| *Assistant:* | How can I help you? |
| *Student:* | I'm having a lot of problems with my roommate. I was wondering if I could possibly move to a single room next semester. |
| *Assistant:* | Probably not. You see, we're really busy this year, and we don't have any empty rooms right now. Ah, maybe you could swap with a friend—we can certainly help you out with that. |
| *Student [unenthusiastically]:* | Possibly. I'd just prefer to live by myself. |
| *Assistant:* | I see. You can definitely complete this form—it's a request for a room transfer. But it's not likely you'll get a single room. |

## Exercise 5.4, Question 3 (page 68). (Track 26)

Listen again to part of the conversation.

| | |
|---|---|
| *Assistant:* | Ah, maybe you could swap with a friend—we can certainly help you out with that. |
| *Student [unenthusiastically]:* | Possibly. I'd just prefer to live by myself. |

## Exercise 5.6 (page 70). (Track 27)

Listen to the conversation between a student and her professor.

*Student (F):*    Dr. Webber, can I ask you about a problem? It's kind of personal.

*Professor (M):* Sure, what's wrong?

*F:*    It's our final group project. I'm having difficulties with one of my groupmates.

*M:*    What kind of difficulties?

*F:*    Well, for a start, finding a time to meet is a big issue. He never seems to have time. And the topic of our project presents a real challenge—we have completely different opinions about the business model.

*M:*    Surely that will make for an interesting presentation!

*F:*    Yeah, but what if he doesn't do the preparation work? It's a really big issue for me! He has no interest in the project, which is really problematic.

## Exercise 5.8 (page 73). (Track 28)

Listen to the lecture.

*Professor:*    An Austrian doctor named Sigmund Freud proposed a solution to the problem of shellshock. He suggested that soldiers with shellshock were living the war again in their heads. This explains why they did not behave normally. To fix the problem, he suggested a talking cure. Soldiers who talked about their experiences in the war could sometimes resolve their problems.

## Exercise 5.9 (page 74). (Track 29)

Listen to the conversation between two students.

*Student (M):*    Hey, Jenny, what's up?

*Student (F):*    I'm worried about the final, Zach.

*M:*    But you're getting an A in the class. You've got nothing to worry about.

*F:*    Yeah, I know, but I've got a different kind of problem. My parents want me to come home for my grandmother's 90th birthday, and it's the same day as the final exam.

*M:*    I see your difficulty. What are you gonna do about it?

| | |
|---|---|
| *F:* | I could just skip the final and get a lower grade. |
| *M:* | No! That's not a good solution! Maybe you can talk to the professor and see if he has a better fix. |
| *F:* | What can I ask him? If I talk to Professor James, I have to suggest some answers. |
| *M:* | He might let you take the final early, before you leave town. |
| *F:* | That's a good idea. Or maybe he can give me another paper to write instead of a final. |

## Exercise 5.10 (page 75). (Track 30)

Listen to the sentences.

1. You can see the effects of global warming.
2. There can't be an easy solution.
3. We can try to use less energy.
4. Most people can't stop driving altogether.
5. Big companies can make a difference.

## Exercise 5.11 (page 76). (Track 31)

Listen to the lecture about drinking and driving laws in the United States.

| | |
|---|---|
| *Professor:* | As you probably all know, you can't drink alcohol in the United States before the age of 21 years old. Right? However, each state can choose that age limit. The main problem is that the federal government can't give money for road building to states with a drinking age lower than 21. Do you understand? For example, Michigan can lower the drinking age to 18. But Michigan then gets no money to fix the roads. In theory, of course, Michigan can pay for its own roads. However, in reality, the state cannot do that because it doesn't have enough money. |

## Exercise 5.12 (page 77). (Track 32)

Listen to the sentences.

1. Today's lecture is about Shakespeare: his life, his theater, and his plays.

2. There are three solutions to this problem: increase education, lower the requirements, or employ foreign workers.

3. Nuclear energy presents three major challenges: storing the waste product, securing the power plants, and protecting the population.

4. Salary, discipline, and testing are the three biggest problems for today's teachers.

5. A business can fail in many ways—it can choose the wrong location, it can set its prices badly, it can hire the wrong people, and it can promote itself poorly.

# Unit 6: Preferences and Opinions

## Exercise 6.3 (page 82). (Track 33)

Listen to two students discussing the announcement.

*Student (F):*   Look at this announcement about the new noise rules.

*Student (M):*   I've seen it. It's crazy. If there are five people in a room, you don't have to be quiet? Even two people can make a lot of noise, you know.

*F:*   Yeah, and what about the music rule. What do they mean: "Residents should not disturb their neighbors"? Is this a rule?

*M:*   I don't think so. I think it's about good manners.

*F:*   Hmm. So, how loud is "too loud"? Who decides? I don't understand this new policy at all!

*M:*   You know the rule I want to see? Cell phones must be turned off at night. I can't sleep because of all the ring tones on my floor.

## Exercise 6.3, Question 3 (page 82). (Track 34)

Listen again to part of the conversation.

*F:*   Yeah, and what about the music rule. What do they mean: "Residents should not disturb their neighbors"? Is this a rule?

*M:*   I don't think so. I think it's about good manners.

## Exercise 6.6 (page 87). (Track 35)

Listen to the lecture about language learning.

*Professor (M):* There are two strong positions on teaching grammar to second language learners. Some people argue that grammar teaching is necessary. They believe that learners will not reach a high level of language without direct grammar teaching. We call this the *direct grammar* approach. On the other hand, some experts claim that we don't have to teach grammar. They think that we should only teach communication skills. This is called *communicative language teaching*. Fortunately, we do not need to choose between these two positions. In my experience, learners want to know about the grammar of a language, so I believe that we should teach some grammar. I have also realized that language must be useful, so I suggest that we teach grammar *for* communication. Unfortunately, the experts rarely agree on this middle opinion!

## Exercise 6.10 (pages 91–92). (Track 36)

Listen to the conversation between a student and her professor.

*Student (F):*  Dr. Lowry, do you think I should go abroad next semester or stay here and finish the requirements for my major?

*Professor (M):*  Well, I guess you could finish your requirements and graduate next semester. But maybe you'd miss out on a new experience.

*F:*  What do you mean?

*M:*  Don't you think your life experiences are kind of limited right now? I mean, you've never even lived outside the state of Virginia.

*F:*  I guess. Do you think it would sort of broaden my mind to study abroad?

*M:*  Yes, I do. Actually, I took a year off from my undergraduate degree to work as a waiter in Spain!

*F:*  It's just . . . well, I don't know how to say this. It's just, I'm worried about getting a job. All my classmates will graduate before me.

*M:*  That's true. But perhaps you will be a somewhat better candidate for a job if you have a little experience of living in another country.

## Exercise 6.10, Question 3 (page 92). (Track 37)

Listen again to part of the conversation.

*Professor:*  Well, I guess you could finish your requirements and graduate next semester. But maybe you'd miss out on a new experience.

## Exercise 6.10, Question 4 (page 92). (Track 38)

Listen again to another part of the conversation.

*Student:*      It's just . . . well, I don't know how to say this. It's just, I'm worried about getting a job. All my classmates will graduate before me.

## Exercise 6.11 (page 93). (Track 39)

Listen to the extracts.

1. [unsure] I don't know. I guess that *might* work.

2. [enthusiastic] That's a great idea! I'll go talk to my advisor right away.

3. [sympathetic] I see your problem. Let me see what I can do.

4. [frustrated] I've sent three emails already, and he never replies!

5. [apologetic] I can't give you your papers today. I had to go a funeral this weekend.

## Exercise 6.13 (page 95). (Track 40)

Listen to the conversation between a student and an assistant in the registrar's office.

*Student (F):*  Um . . . hi. Um, I have a question about my tuition fees.

*Assistant (M):* I'm sorry, we don't answer questions in person.

*F:*          Oh, um, I see. Ah, well then, how can I ask my question?

*M:*        You need to send us an email, and we'll get back to you in, oh, 48 hours.

*F:*          Oh, um, that's a problem. Uh, the bill is due tomorrow, and I think there's been a mistake.

*M:*        Well, alright. I'll take a look at it. Oh no, that's not right. It should be $100, not $1,000.

*F:*          Oh, wow! That's a big difference.

## Exercise 6.14 (page 95). (Track 41)

Take the part of the student, and finish the conversation. (Pauses are provided on the audio.)

*Advisor:*      What subject would you like to major in?

*Advisor:*      Why did you choose that?

*Advisor:*      What would you like to do after college?

*Advisor:*      Do you have any questions about your classes for next year?

# Unit 7: Paraphrasing

## Exercise 7.4 (page 100). (Track 42)

Listen to the lecture.

*Professor:*    Mackinac Island is a major tourist attraction in Michigan. It is located between Lake Michigan and Lake Huron. Cars are not allowed on the island, so you can choose between two types of transportation: bikes and horses! You get to the island by ferry—it runs between May and October. But there are still a few residents on the island in the winter. These people need to take a plane to the mainland.

## Exercise 7.10 (page 106). (Track 43)

Listen to the professor talk about price controls.

*Professor:*    So, you've all read in your textbooks about price controls. The problem with price controls is that they don't work. If the profit margin—that means the amount of profit a company makes on the sale of their product—if the profit margin is too small, then companies will stop making the product, or the quality might decrease. As a result, there may be a shortage, or a lack of the product, which will push the price higher.

## Exercise 7.13 (page 111). (Track 44)

Listen to the correct pauses and intonation.

1. The American Revolution, which happened in 1776, marks the birth of the United States.

2. Britain, which had controlled America, went to war as a result.

3. An army leader, who was called George Washington, became the first president.

4. There were still people who wanted to be part of Britain.

5. The Americans won the war, which is known today as the War of Independence.

## Exercise 7.15 (page 113). (Track 45)

Listen to the words.

| | | | | | | |
|---|---|---|---|---|---|---|
| eats | reads | watches | chooses | books | goes | has |
| wakes | rides | studies | advises | says | tells | writes |

## Exercise 7.16 (page 114). (Track 46)

Listen to the correct pronunciation.

> The professor explains that he often catches colds on airplanes. He says that germs in the air spread diseases. However, the author disagrees with this opinion. He argues that no one gets sick from air travel. The research supports his claims.

# Unit 8: Sources of Information

## Exercise 8.2 (page 118). (Track 47)

Listen to the lecture.

> *Professor (M):* Single-sex schools do not provide the same social experience as mixed schools. Therefore, although their test scores may be higher, students from single-sex schools may have greater problems adjusting to college life (unless they go to a single-sex college, of course). Some studies suggest that boys do better in mixed schools because the girls motivate them. Girls also benefit because they learn from the boys not to worry so much about tests, and so they can be less nervous and can have fewer emotional problems.

## Exercise 8.6 (page 122). (Track 48)

Listen to the lecture about microwave ovens.

> *Professor (F):* There have been a lot of questions about the safety of microwave ovens, or microwaves for short. For example, your textbook says that it is not safe to put any plastic containers in the microwave. This is not good advice. Research has showed that some plastics are dangerous because they can melt in the microwave. But most experts say that it is okay to use microwave-safe plastics. Again, your textbook

suggests that all plastics release harmful chemicals into your food. However, scientists say that the quantities are too small to be dangerous. I think that we can continue using microwave-safe containers, but we should not use them all the time.

## Exercise 8.9 (pages 124–26). (Track 49)

Listen to the lecture.

*Professor (M):* I want to present the opposite side to the nature argument you read about in your books. What is the other explanation for personality development?

*Student (F):* Is it nurture?

*M:* Exactly, nurture. Nobody disagrees that DNA—genes—determine physical characteristics. But the results of genetic personality research are not so clear. The nature side argues that environment forms personality. Let's take shyness. If children do not receive love and affection at an early age, then it doesn't matter if they have a genetic tendency to be outgoing. They often grow up to be shy and distrustful. What about musical ability? Obviously, if you have this gene and you never practice the piano, you won't be a concert piano player! And as for crime, the genetic research doesn't prove anything. Some kids who have the so-called crime gene don't become criminals, and others do. So there must be environmental factors at work here, too. I think, therefore, that both nature and nurture play a role in personality development.

## Exercise 8.10 (page 127). (Track 50)

Listen to the words.

that    think    their    the    author    health

## Exercise 8.11 (page 127). (Track 51)

Listen to the correct pronunciation.

The author's opinion is that the Earth is getting warmer because of the thinning of the ozone layer. This is thought to be dangerous for health because thermal rays from the sun can reach the Earth, thus causing skin cancer. However, the lecturer thinks that this theory is incorrect. Even though he accepts that the Earth is getting warmer, there have been other periods of increased warmth in history, he says. In 30 years' time, those scientists like him might be thought to be telling the truth.

## Exercise 8.12 (page 129). (Track 52)

Listen to the extracts.

1. *Advisor (F):*   You need to take this form to the administration building. Do you know where that is?

2. *Professor (M):*   Today we're going to talk about a key concept in economics: capitalism. So, what is capitalism? Well, according to Smith, capitalism is defined as . . . .

3. *Student (F):*   James, have you done your math homework?

   *Student (M):*   Not yet. When is it due?

   *Student (F):*   Today. You'd better hurry up!

4. *Professor (M):*   The article you read for homework argued that babies should learn sign language. But is this really good advice? Let's look at the claims made about sign language and ask if they are right.

5. *Student (F):*   Professor, I don't understand your comment on my last paper. I wrote, "American students leave home at the age of 18."

   *Professor (M):*   *All* American students leave home at age 18? *No one* lives at home while they attend college or start a job?

   *Student (F):*   Oh, I guess that's not true for everyone.

## Exercise 8.13 (page 130). (Track 53)

Listen to the correct question forms.

1. Why do universities operate like businesses?

2. Do recycling programs save energy?

3. Which metals are the best conductors of electricity?

4. How do trees help to clean the air?

5. Is non-verbal communication more important than verbal communication?

## Exercise 8.14 (page 131). (Track 54)

Listen to the answer.

Conflict means a problem or argument between people. How can we resolve a conflict? There are two ways to resolve a conflict: *contending* and *yielding*. What is contending? Contending means that a third person makes a decision about how to end the conflict. For example, your parents might tell you and your sister to stop fighting. Does it work? No, it doesn't always work because you might both be unhappy with the solution. What is the second strategy? The other strategy is called *yielding*. Yielding is when you choose to lose the argument. Why might you do this? You might do this because you don't want to create a bad feeling with someone. So, one strategy is better than the other? I don't think there is one right answer: it depends on the conflict.